Exploring Fractions:
Mastering Fractional Concepts & Operations

By
KARISE MACE & AMY DOVERSPIKE

D1495873

COPYRIGHT © 2008 Mark Twain Media, Inc.

ISBN 978-1-58037-447-7

Printing No. CD-404088

Mark Twain Media, Inc., Publishers
Distributed by Carson-Dellosa Publishing Company, Inc.

Table of Contents

Letter From the Authors

We are so glad that you have purchased *Exploring Fractions: Mastering Fractional Concepts and Operations.* This book is divided into five units covering fractional concepts from the basics to operations with fractions and mixed numbers. A unit is divided into several lessons, each of which covers one or two concepts.

You will notice that each lesson is made up of three parts. The first part, called "Let's EXPLORE!", is a teacher-guided exploration that is hands-on. The goal of this part of the lesson is to help students understand the *why* of the particular fraction concept being covered by using real-life context. The second part, called "Let's EXERCISE!", is a set of exercises where students can practice the concepts they learned in the exploration. The third part, called "Show Your EXPERTISE!", is an activity, small project, or set of critical-thinking questions that asks the students to apply what they have learned about the concepts covered in the lesson. This part of the lesson could be used as an assessment to help the teacher evaluate what the students have learned.

Each unit also contains a page or two of teacher notes. In these pages, we have made suggestions on how to make the explorations run smoothly as well as paper and pencil alternatives for the activities that require extra materials.

We have also provided an alignment to show you how this book addresses the Number and Operation Standard of the NCTM standards.

We hope that you and your students will have fun exploring fractions!

Mathematically yours,

Karise Mace and Amy Doverspike

Alignment to NCTM Number and Operation Standard

Expectations	Unit 1	Unit 2	Unit 3	Unit 4	Unit 5
Number and Operation Standard					
Students should understand numbers, ways of representing numbers, relationships among numbers, and number systems.					
Students should work flexibly with fractions, decimals, and percents to solve problems.	•	•	•	•	•
Students should compare and order fractions, decimals, and percents efficiently and find their approximate locations on a number line.	•				
Students should develop meaning for percents greater than 100 and less than 1.					
Students should understand and use ratios and proportions to represent quantitative relationships.					
Students should develop an understanding of large numbers and recognize and appropriately use exponential, scientific, and calculator notation.					
Students should use factors, multiples, prime factorization, and relatively prime numbers to solve problems.		•			
Students should develop meaning for integers and represent and compare quantities with them.					
Students should understand meanings of operations and how they relate to one another.					
Students should understand the meaning and effects of arithmetic operations with fractions, decimals, and integers.		•	•	•	•
Students should use the associative and commutative properties of addition and multiplication and the distributive property of multiplication over addition to simplify computations with integers, fractions, and decimals.					
Students should understand and use the inverse relationships of addition and subtraction, multiplication and division, and squaring and finding square roots to simplify computations and solve problems.					
Students should compute fluently and make reasonable estimates.					
Students should select appropriate methods and tools for computing with fractions and decimals from among mental computation, estimation, calculators or computers, and paper and pencil, depending on the situation, and apply the selected methods.		•	•	•	•
Students should develop and analyze algorithms for computing with fractions, decimals, and integers and develop fluency in their use.		•	•	•	•
Students should develop and use strategies to estimate the results of rational-number computations and judge the reasonableness of the results.					
Students should develop, analyze, and explain methods for solving problems involving proportions, such as scaling and finding equivalent ratios.					

Unit 1: The Basics

Teacher Notes

Understanding Fractions

Let's EXPLORE!

A paper-pencil alternative for using real fruit is to use the pictures of fruit on the following page. Allowing students to color their fruit will engage them more in the lesson.

Equivalent Fractions

Let's EXPLORE!

A paper-pencil alternative for using the candy bar is to use the picture of the bar on the following page.

Simplifying Fractions

Let's EXPLORE!

A paper-pencil alternative for using the fish crackers is to use the pictures of the fish on the following page.

Comparing and Ordering Fractions

Let's EXPLORE!

A paper-pencil alternative for using the fruity cereal is to use the pictures on the next page. Make sure to copy them onto colored paper. If there is no colored paper to copy on, you may want the students to color the cereal pieces.

Grapes

Orange slices

Candy Bar

Fish Crackers

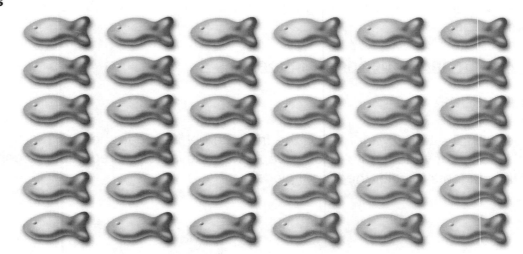

Fruity Cereal

Name: _Kamron Bourne_____ Date: _3-24-2014_____

Unit 1: The Basics—Understanding Fractions

Let's EXPLORE!

Materials:
- ☑ small bunch of grapes (at least 10 grapes on the bunch)
- ☑ 1 citrus fruit, such as an orange, tangerine, or Clementine

Vocabulary:
- ↳ fraction
- ↳ numerator
- ↳ denominator

A **fraction** is defined as a part of a group or a part of a whole.

Fractions are written as one number over another number. The top number is known as the **numerator**, and the bottom number is known as the **denominator**.

What does all of this mean exactly? Let's go on an exploration and figure it out!

First, we'll explore fractions as a part of a group.

1. How many grapes are in your bunch? __14__

2. Pull several grapes off the bunch to eat. How many did you pull off? __5__

3. Use your answers to Questions 1 and 2 to write the fraction of grapes you pulled off to eat. Then eat the grapes you pulled off.

$$\frac{\text{number of grapes to eat}}{\text{total grapes}} = \frac{5}{14}$$

4. How many grapes do you have left? __9__

5. Use your answers to Questions 1 and 4 to write the fraction of grapes you have left.

$$\frac{\text{number of grapes left}}{\text{total grapes}} = \frac{9}{14}$$

Name: _____ Date: _____

Unit 1: The Basics—Understanding Fractions (cont.)

Now, let's explore fractions as a part of a whole.

6. Peel your citrus fruit and divide it into segments.

7. How many segments do you have? ____6____

8. Put aside several segments to eat. How many did you put aside? ____3____

9. Use your answers to Questions 7 and 8 to write the fraction of your fruit you put aside to eat. Then eat these segments.

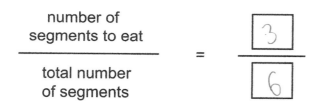

number of
segments to eat
_____   = $\dfrac{3}{6}$
total number
of segments

10. How many segments do you have left? ____3____

11. Use your answers to Questions 7 and 10 to write the fraction of your fruit that you have left.

number of
segments left
_____   = $\dfrac{3}{6}$
total number
of segments

Now, enjoy eating your fruit while you answer the following questions.

12. Why were the grapes used to show a fraction as part of a group? Use complete sentences in your answer.

   Because they are easy and simple to
   follow and always come in pairs.

13. Why was the citrus fruit used to show a fraction as part of a whole? Use complete sentences in your answer.

   Because the orange is already part of
   a whole and it can be separated into
   smaller segments.

4

Unit 1: The Basics—Understanding Fractions (cont.)

Let's EXERCISE!

Fractions as Parts of a Group
Write a fraction that names how many in each set are circled.

1. $\dfrac{3}{6}$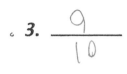

2. $\dfrac{4}{9}$

3. $\dfrac{9}{10}$

4. $\dfrac{5}{11}$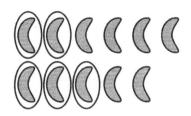

Fractions as Part of a Whole
Write a fraction that names the shaded part of each picture.

5. $\dfrac{6}{8}$

6. $\dfrac{2}{5}$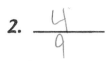

7. $\dfrac{9}{11}$

8. $\dfrac{1}{4}$

Extend Your Knowledge!

9. Draw a picture that shows $\dfrac{3}{5}$ as parts of a group.

10. Draw a picture that shows $\dfrac{3}{5}$ as part of a whole.

Unit 1: The Basics—Understanding Fractions (cont.)

Show your EXPERTISE!

Fractions as Parts of a Group

You are going to make a fruit salad. Use the fruit salad to answer each question.

1. You would like 15 pieces of fruit in your bowl. Determine the number of pieces of each fruit below that you are going to put in your bowl so that the total is 15. Then draw the fruit in your bowl.

   __5__ strawberries

   __6__ chunks of pineapple

   __4__ cherries

2. What fraction of your fruit salad is strawberries? __$\frac{5}{15}$__

3. What fraction of your fruit salad is chunks of pineapple? __$\frac{6}{15}$__

4. What fraction of your fruit salad is cherries? __$\frac{4}{15}$__

5. What fraction of your fruit salad is strawberries and chunks of pineapple? __$\frac{11}{15}$__

6. What fraction of your fruit salad is strawberries and cherries? __$\frac{9}{15}$__

Fractions as Part of a Whole

You are going to make a paper fruit pizza. Use the pizza to answer each question.

7. Draw slices of kiwi on $\frac{3}{8}$ of your pizza.

   How many pieces have kiwi slices on them? __$\frac{3}{8}$__

8. Draw blueberries on $\frac{7}{8}$ of your pizza.

   How many pieces have blueberries on them? __$\frac{7}{8}$__

9. Draw slices of peaches on $\frac{4}{8}$ of your pizza.

   How many pieces have peaches on them? __$\frac{4}{8}$__

10. What fraction of your pizza has slices of kiwi and peaches? __$\frac{7}{8}$__

11. What fraction of your pizza has slices of peaches and blueberries? __$1\frac{3}{8}$__

12. What fraction of your pizza has all three toppings? __$\frac{6}{8}$__

Unit 1: The Basics—Understanding Fractions (cont.)

Show your EXPERTISE!

Fractions as Parts of a Group

You are going to make a fruit salad. Use the fruit salad to answer each question.

1. You would like 15 pieces of fruit in your bowl. Determine the number of pieces of each fruit below that you are going to put in your bowl so that the total is 15. Then draw the fruit in your bowl.

    _____ strawberries

    _____ chunks of pineapple

    _____ cherries

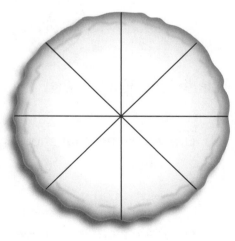

2. What fraction of your fruit salad is strawberries? _____

3. What fraction of your fruit salad is chunks of pineapple? _____

4. What fraction of your fruit salad is cherries? _____

5. What fraction of your fruit salad is strawberries and chunks of pineapple? _____

6. What fraction of your fruit salad is strawberries and cherries? _____

Fractions as Part of a Whole

You are going to make a paper fruit pizza. Use the pizza to answer each question.

7. Draw slices of kiwi on $\frac{3}{8}$ of your pizza.

    How many pieces have kiwi slices on them? _____

8. Draw blueberries on $\frac{7}{8}$ of your pizza.

    How many pieces have blueberries on them? _____

9. Draw slices of peaches on $\frac{4}{8}$ of your pizza.

    How many pieces have peaches on them? _____

10. What fraction of your pizza has slices of kiwi and peaches? _____

11. What fraction of your pizza has slices of peaches and blueberries? _____

12. What fraction of your pizza has all three toppings? _____

Name: _____   Date: _____

Unit 1: The Basics—Understanding Fractions (cont.)

Let's EXERCISE!

Fractions as Parts of a Group

Write a fraction that names how many in each set are circled.

1. _____

2. _____

3. _____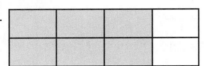

4. _____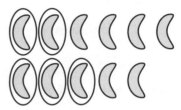

Fractions as Part of a Whole

Write a fraction that names the shaded part of each picture.

5. _____

6. _____

7. _____

8. _____

Extend Your Knowledge!

9. Draw a picture that shows $\frac{3}{5}$ as parts of a group.

10. Draw a picture that shows $\frac{3}{5}$ as part of a whole.

Name: _____ Date: _____

Unit 1: The Basics—Understanding Fractions (cont.)

Now, let's explore fractions as a part of a whole.

6. Peel your citrus fruit and divide it into segments.

7. How many segments do you have? _____

8. Put aside several segments to eat. How many did you put aside? _____

9. Use your answers to Questions 7 and 8 to write the fraction of your fruit you put aside to eat. Then eat these segments.

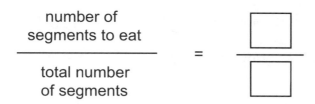 

10. How many segments do you have left? _____

11. Use your answers to Questions 7 and 10 to write the fraction of your fruit that you have left.

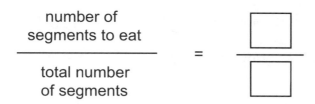

Now, enjoy eating your fruit while you answer the following questions.

12. Why were the grapes used to show a fraction as part of a group? Use complete sentences in your answer.

_____

_____

13. Why was the citrus fruit used to show a fraction as part of a whole? Use complete sentences in your answer.

_____

_____

Name: _____ Date: _____

 ## Unit 1: The Basics—Understanding Fractions

Let's EXPLORE!

Materials:
- ☐ small bunch of grapes (at least 10 grapes on the bunch)
- ☐ 1 citrus fruit, such as an orange, tangerine, or Clementine

Vocabulary:
- ↳ fraction
- ↳ numerator
- ↳ denominator

A **fraction** is defined as a part of a group or a part of a whole.

Fractions are written as one number over another number. The top number is known as the **numerator**, and the bottom number is known as the **denominator**.

What does all of this mean exactly? Let's go on an exploration and figure it out!

First, we'll explore fractions as a part of a group.

1. How many grapes are in your bunch? _____

2. Pull several grapes off the bunch to eat. How many did you pull off? _____

3. Use your answers to Questions 1 and 2 to write the fraction of grapes you pulled off to eat. Then eat the grapes you pulled off.

$$\frac{\text{number of grapes to eat}}{\text{total grapes}} = \frac{\boxed{}}{\boxed{}}$$

4. How many grapes do you have left? _____

5. Use your answers to Questions 1 and 4 to write the fraction of grapes you have left.

$$\frac{\text{number of grapes left}}{\text{total grapes}} = \frac{\boxed{}}{\boxed{}}$$

Name: _____ Date: _____

Unit 1: The Basics—Equivalent Fractions

Let's EXPLORE!

Materials:
  ❑ one 12-piece chocolate bar

Vocabulary:
  ☞ equivalent

Equivalent is another word for equal.

Let's talk chocolate! Work through the questions before your chocolate melts!

1. How many small rectangles make up the chocolate bar? _____

2. Break the chocolate bar into halves, making two equal parts. How many small rectangles are in one of the halves? _____

3. Use your answers from Questions 1 and 2 to write a fraction that is equivalent to $\frac{1}{2}$ of the chocolate bar.

$$\frac{\text{number of small rectangles in one half}}{\text{total of small rectangles in the whole bar}} = \frac{\boxed{}}{\boxed{}}$$

Lay the pieces of the chocolate bar side by side so it is whole again to complete Questions 4 and 5.

4. Break the chocolate bar into thirds by making three equal parts. How many small rectangles are in one of the thirds? _____

5. Use your answers from Questions 1 and 4 to write a fraction that is equivalent to $\frac{1}{3}$ of the chocolate bar.

$$\frac{\text{number of small rectangles in one third}}{\text{total of small rectangles in the whole bar}} = \frac{\boxed{}}{\boxed{}}$$

Name: _____   Date: _____

Unit 1: The Basics—Equivalent Fractions (cont.)

Lay the pieces of the chocolate bar side by side so it is whole again to complete Questions 6 and 7.

6. Break the chocolate bar into fourths by making four equal parts. How many small rectangles are in one of the four parts? _____

7. Use your answers from Questions 1 and 6 to write a fraction that is equivalent to $\frac{1}{4}$ of the chocolate bar.

$$\frac{\text{number of small rectangles in one fourth}}{\text{total of small rectangles in the whole bar}} = \frac{\boxed{}}{\boxed{}}$$

Now, have some chocolate while you answer the following questions.

8. How would you define what equivalent fractions are using the information from our exploration? Use complete sentences in your answer.

_____

_____

_____

_____

_____

9. How did breaking the chocolate bar into fractional pieces help us find an equivalent fraction? Use complete sentences in your answer.

_____

_____

_____

_____

Name: _____ Date: _____

Unit 1: The Basics–Equivalent Fractions (cont.)

Let's EXERCISE!

Writing Equivalent Fractions

Write two equivalent fractions that represent the shaded part of each picture.

1. _____ _____

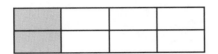

2. _____ _____

3. _____ _____

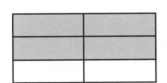

4. _____ _____

Draw a picture with rectangles to represent the fraction, and then write an equivalent fraction.

5. $\frac{4}{10}$ _____

6. $\frac{5}{15}$ _____

7. $\frac{2}{12}$ _____

8. $\frac{4}{16}$ _____

Extend Your Knowledge!

9. How many equivalent fractions can be written for $\frac{1}{1}$? Explain why, using complete sentences.

_____

_____

_____

Name: _____ Date: _____

Unit 1: The Basics—Equivalent Fractions (cont.)

Show Your EXPERTISE!

Writing Equivalent Fractions

You are going to share three candy bars and one roll of caramels with your friends. Use the candy bars and caramels to answer each question.

1. You and a friend are going to share a candy bar that has 4 total pieces. To be fair, you and your friend should have the same number of pieces. Draw the candy bar with your share shaded in one color and your friend's share in another color.

2. What two equivalent fractions of the candy bar did you share with your friend?

   _____ _____

3. You and two friends are going to share a candy bar that has 6 total pieces. To be fair, everybody should have the same number of pieces. Draw the candy bar, shading everybody's share differently.

4. What two equivalent fractions of the candy bar did each person get? _____ _____

5. You and a friend are going to share an 8-piece roll of caramels. Your friend would like 2 caramels. Draw the roll of caramels with your pieces shaded.

6. What two equivalent fractions represent your pieces? _____ _____

Name: _____ Date: _____

Unit 1: The Basics—Simplifying Fractions

Let's EXPLORE!

Materials:
- ❑ 36 fish crackers

Vocabulary:
- ✎ factor
- ✎ common factor
- ✎ simplify

When two numbers are multiplied together, the result is a product. The two numbers that were used to find the product are called **factors**.

A **common factor** is a factor that two numbers share.

To **simplify** a fraction, you must divide out the common factors from the numerator and the denominator.

Let's swim through this exploration to learn about simplifying fractions.

1. How many total fish crackers do you have? _____

2. Divide your fish crackers in half by making 2 equal piles. How many are in each half?

   _____

3. Use your answers from Questions 1 and 2 to write a fraction that represents the number of fish crackers in one of the 2 piles.

   number of fish crackers in
   one of the 2 piles
   _____ = _____
   total number
   of fish crackers

4. How does the fraction you made in Question 3 compare to the fraction of $\frac{1}{2}$? Use complete

   sentences in your answer. _____

   _____

   _____

5. What number was divided out of the numerator in Question 3 to get 1? _____

11

Name: _____ Date: _____

Unit 1: The Basics—Simplifying Fractions (cont.)

6. What number was divided out of the denominator in Question 3 to get 2? _____

7. What is the common factor that was divided out of the fraction from Question 3 to simplify the fraction to $\frac{1}{2}$? _____

Put the fish crackers back into one pile for Questions 8–13.

8. Divide up your fish crackers into thirds by making 3 equal piles. How many are in each pile? _____

9. Use your answers from Questions 1 and 8 to write a fraction that represents the number of fish crackers in one of the 3 piles.

$$\frac{\text{number of fish crackers in one of the 3 piles}}{\text{total number of fish crackers}} = \frac{\boxed{}}{\boxed{}}$$

10. How does the fraction you made in Question 9 compare to the fraction of $\frac{1}{3}$? Use complete sentences in your answer. _____

_____

_____

11. What number was divided out of the numerator in Question 9 to get 1? _____

12. What number was divided out of the denominator in Question 9 to get 3? _____

13. What is the common factor that was divided out of the fraction in Question 9 to simply the fraction down to $\frac{1}{3}$? _____

Help yourself to some fish crackers while you come up for air to answer the following questions. Write the answers on your own paper, and use complete sentences in your answers.

14. How are equivalent fractions related to simplifying fractions?

15. How do you find the largest common factor to divide out of the numerator and the denominator?

Name: _____   Date: _____

Unit 1: The Basics—Simplifying Fractions (cont.)

Let's EXERCISE!

Finding the Greatest Common Factor

Find the greatest common factor between the two given numbers.

1. 4 and 12 _____

2. 2 and 18 _____

3. 10 and 25 _____

4. 9 and 21 _____

Simplifying Fractions

Find the fraction that represents the shaded region in the pictures. Write the fraction in simplified form.

5. _____

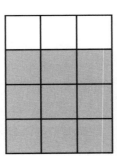

6. _____

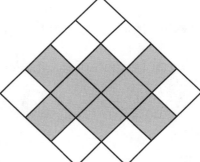

7. _____

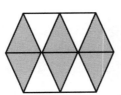

8. _____

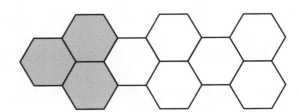

Extend Your Knowledge!

9. How do you know when a fraction is as simplified as possible? Use complete sentences in your answer. _____

_____

_____

Name: _____ Date: _____

Unit 1: The Basics—Simplifying Fractions (cont.)

Show Your EXPERTISE!

Simplifying Fractions

You are going to have a party where you serve rainbow fish crackers and pretzel fish crackers as snacks. There are going to be big bowls of fish crackers to share and gift bags filled with fish crackers for your guests to take with them at the end of the party.

One of the bowls is going to have a mixture of fish crackers. There are going to be 15 pretzel, 5 red, 8 purple, 10 orange, 5 yellow, and 7 green fish crackers in the bowl. Use the numbers of fish crackers to write the fractions in simplest form.

1. What fraction of the fish crackers in the bowl are pretzel? _____

2. What fraction of the fish crackers in the bowl are red? _____

3. What fraction of the fish crackers in the bowl are purple? _____

4. What fraction of the fish crackers in the bowl are orange? _____

5. What fraction of the fish crackers in the bowl are yellow? _____

6. What fraction of the fish crackers in the bowl are green? _____

The gift bags for your guests are going to have a mixture of fish crackers as well. There are going to be 5 pretzel, 2 red, 2 purple, 3 yellow, and 8 green fish crackers in each bag. Use the number of fish crackers to write the fractions in simplest form.

7. What fraction of the fish crackers in the bag are pretzel? _____

8. What fraction of the fish crackers in the bag are red? _____

9. What fraction of the fish crackers in the bag are purple? _____

10. What fraction of the fish crackers in the bag are yellow? _____

11. What fraction of the fish crackers in the bag are green? _____

Name: _____ Date: _____

Unit 1: The Basics—Comparing and Ordering Fractions

Let's EXPLORE!

Materials:
- ❑ fruity cereal pieces:
  2 yellow, 10 blue, 5 orange, 3 green

Vocabulary:
- ↳ descending order
- ↳ ascending order
- ↳ common denominator

Descending order is arranged from biggest to smallest.

Ascending order is arranged from smallest to biggest.

A **common denominator** is a multiple of all the denominators.

Let's pick through the exploration to learn about simplifying fractions!

1. How many pieces of each color do you have?

   Yellow _____   Blue _____   Orange _____   Green _____

2. How many total pieces do you have? _____

3. Use your answers from Questions 1 and 2 to write fractions that represent how many pieces of each color there are in your group. The second fraction should be simplified.

$$\frac{\text{total number of yellow pieces}}{\text{total number of pieces}} = \frac{\boxed{}}{\boxed{}} = \frac{\boxed{}}{\boxed{}} \qquad \frac{\text{total number of blue pieces}}{\text{total number of pieces}} = \frac{\boxed{}}{\boxed{}} = \frac{\boxed{}}{\boxed{}}$$

$$\frac{\text{total number of orange pieces}}{\text{total number of pieces}} = \frac{\boxed{}}{\boxed{}} = \frac{\boxed{}}{\boxed{}} \qquad \frac{\text{total number of green pieces}}{\text{total number of pieces}} = \frac{\boxed{}}{\boxed{}} = \frac{\boxed{}}{\boxed{}}$$

Unit 1: The Basics—Comparing and Ordering Fractions (cont.)

4. Which color is most plentiful, and what two equivalent fractions represent that color?

_____

5. Which color is least plentiful, and what two equivalent fractions represent that color?

_____

6. Write two inequalities that compare the fractions of the most plentiful color and the least plentiful color. Use < or > in your answers.

_____

7. Which set of fractions is easier to compare, the original or simplified fractions? Use complete sentences to explain why in your answer.

_____

_____

8. Using the information you know about common denominators, write the simplified fractions of pieces in ascending order.

_____

Pick some pieces of fruit cereal for yourself while you answer the following questions.

9. Why is it important to have common denominators when comparing or ordering fractions? Use complete sentences in your answer.

_____

_____

10. How can you get common denominators in fractions when you compare or order them? Use complete sentences in your answer.

_____

_____

_____

Unit 1: The Basics—Comparing and Ordering Fractions (cont.)

Let's EXERCISE!

Comparing Fractions

Write the fraction that represents each picture, and then write the fractions with common denominators. Use >, <, or = to fill in the circle to compare the fractions.

1.

_____ _____

_____ ◯ _____

2.

_____ _____

_____ ◯ _____

Use >, <, or = to fill in the circle to compare the two fractions in each set.

3. $\frac{1}{3}$ ◯ $\frac{1}{2}$

4. $\frac{2}{5}$ ◯ $\frac{2}{15}$

5. $\frac{3}{4}$ ◯ $\frac{5}{6}$

6. $\frac{2}{7}$ ◯ $\frac{4}{14}$

7. $\frac{9}{10}$ ◯ $\frac{6}{7}$

8. $\frac{11}{25}$ ◯ $\frac{8}{20}$

Ordering Fractions

List the fractions in descending order.

9. $\frac{4}{12}$, $\frac{1}{12}$, $\frac{6}{12}$ _____

10. $\frac{2}{9}$, $\frac{1}{3}$, $\frac{5}{18}$ _____

List the fractions in ascending order.

11. $\frac{4}{7}$, $\frac{1}{7}$, $\frac{6}{7}$ _____

12. $\frac{3}{8}$, $\frac{5}{24}$, $\frac{5}{6}$ _____

Extend Your Knowledge!

13. How can you get fractions with unlike denominators and no common factors to have common denominators? Use complete sentences in your answer.

_____

_____

_____

Name: _____ Date: _____

Unit 1: The Basics—Comparing and Ordering Fractions (cont.)

Show Your EXPERTISE!

Comparing Fractions

You are playing a guessing game with your friends using fruity cereal. One goal of the game is to guess how many pieces of fruit cereal are in the bag. Another goal is to guess how many pieces of each color are in the bag. The cereal has 6 different colors. The bag is made up of $\frac{3}{25}$ red pieces, $\frac{3}{20}$ orange pieces, $\frac{13}{100}$ yellow pieces, $\frac{6}{25}$ green pieces, $\frac{11}{50}$ blue pieces, and $\frac{7}{50}$ purple pieces.

Use the fractions to answer the questions.

1. What color is most plentiful? _____

2. What color is least plentiful? _____

3. Are there more yellow pieces than blue pieces? _____

4. Which color is more plentiful: orange, yellow, or purple? _____

5. Which color is least plentiful: purple or orange? _____

Ordering Fractions

You want to play the same game using a jar of candy-coated chocolate pieces. There are 4 different colors of pieces in the jar. The jar is made up of $\frac{1}{3}$ brown pieces, $\frac{5}{6}$ blue pieces, $\frac{1}{4}$ green pieces, and $\frac{7}{12}$ orange pieces.

Use the fractions to answer the questions.

6. Which color is most plentiful? _____

7. Which color is least plentiful? _____

8. List the colors in descending order. _____

18

Unit 2: Adding and Subtracting Fractions

Teacher Notes

Finding Common Multiples

Let's EXPLORE!

Before beginning this Exploration, you may want to review how to find multiples. You can begin by having the students find the multiples of 1.

Adding and Subtracting Fractions With Unlike Denominators

Show Your EXPERTISE!

Have the students make their flags for the activity. Once they have finished the worksheet, instruct students to embellish their flags. They can come up with country names that incorporate fractional vocabulary. Once the flags have all been decorated, hang them up and let the students do a "flag walk" to see how creative their fellow classmates are.

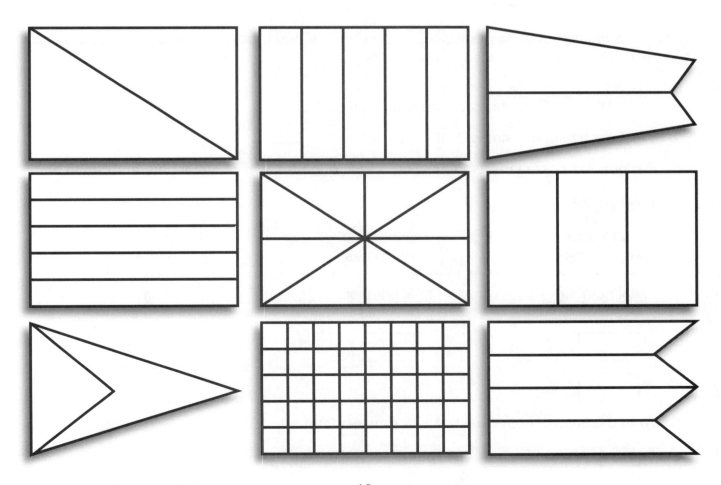

Unit 2: Adding and Subtracting Fractions—Adding and Subtracting Fractions With Like Denominators

Let's EXPLORE!

Materials:
- ❑ Map of the United States of America
- ❑ Blue, purple, green, red, and yellow crayons

Let's use our map of the United States on page 22 to find our way through this exploration!

First, we'll look at addition.

1. Color 9 of the states blue, 17 purple, 11 green, 7 red, and 6 yellow.

2. How many states did you color purple and green? _____

3. Identify what operation is needed to find the total number of states colored purple and green. _____

To find the fraction of states that were colored purple and green, we need to use the same operation. Then we need to identify the fractions.

4. What fraction of the states on the map is purple? _____

5. What fraction of the states on the map is green? _____

6. Perform the operation from Question 3 to find the fraction of states that are purple and green on your map.

number of purple states		number of green states		number of purple and green states
——————————	+	——————————	=	——————————————
total number of states		total number of states		total number of states

$$\frac{\boxed{}}{\boxed{}} \quad + \quad \frac{\boxed{}}{\boxed{}} \quad = \quad \frac{\boxed{}}{\boxed{}}$$

7. Write the answer from Question 6 in simplest form. _____

Name: _____ Date: _____

Unit 2: Adding and Subtracting Fractions—Adding and Subtracting Fractions With Like Denominators (cont.)

Now, let's look at subtraction.

8. How many more states did you color blue than red? _____

9. Identify what operation is needed to find how many more states are blue than red.

_____

To find the fraction of states that are more blue than red, we need to use the same operation. Then we need to identify the fractions.

10. What fraction of the states on the map is blue? _____

11. What fraction of the states on the map is red? _____

12. Perform the operation from Question 9 to find the fraction of states that are more blue than red on your map.

number of blue states		number of red states		number of states that are more blue than red
————————	–	————————	=	————————
total number of states		total number of states		total number of states

$$\frac{\boxed{}}{\boxed{}} - \frac{\boxed{}}{\boxed{}} = \frac{\boxed{}}{\boxed{}}$$

13. Write the answer from Question 12 in simplest form. _____

Look over the exploration to help find your way to the answers!

14. What part of the fractions changed? Why? Use complete sentences in your answer.

_____

_____

15. What part of the fraction stayed the same? Why? Use complete sentences in your answer.

_____

_____

Name: _____ Date: _____

Unit 2: Adding and Subtracting Fractions—Adding and Subtracting Fractions With Like Denominators (cont.)

Let's EXPLORE!

Map of The United States of America

Unit 2: Adding and Subtracting Fractions–Adding and Subtracting Fractions With Like Denominators (cont.)

Let's EXERCISE!

Adding Fractions

Write the fraction represented by the picture, and then add the fractions. Simplify your answer when necessary.

1.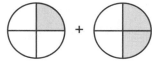

_____ + _____ = _____

2.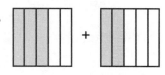

_____ + _____ = _____

Add the fractions. Simplify your answer when necessary.

3. $\frac{5}{15} + \frac{4}{15} =$ _____   **4.** $\frac{3}{8} + \frac{2}{8} =$ _____   **5.** $\frac{6}{21} + \frac{7}{21} =$ _____

Subtracting Fractions

Write the fraction represented by the picture, and then subtract the fractions. Simplify your answer when necessary.

6.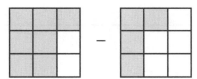

_____ – _____ = _____

7.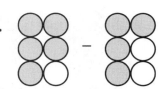

_____ – _____ = _____

Subtract the fractions. Simplify your answer when necessary.

8. $\frac{9}{10} - \frac{3}{10} =$ _____   **9.** $\frac{7}{11} - \frac{3}{11} =$ _____   **10.** $\frac{5}{17} - \frac{4}{17}$ _____

Extend Your Knowledge!

11. What type of answer will you get if the second fraction is larger than the first fraction in a subtraction problem?

_____

Name: _____ Date: _____

Unit 2: Adding and Subtracting Fractions—Adding and Subtracting Fractions With Like Denominators (cont.)

Show Your EXPERTISE!

Adding and Subtracting Fractions With Like Denominators

On your map of Oregon, color 7 counties blue, 10 counties purple, 8 counties green, 9 counties red, and 2 counties yellow. Use the map to answer the questions.

For 1–5, do not simplify the fractions.

1. What fraction of the map is blue? _____

2. What fraction of the map is purple? _____

3. What fraction of the map is green? _____

4. What fraction of the map is red? _____

5. What fraction of the map is yellow? _____

For 6–11, write out the fractions in an addition or subtraction problem, and then simplify your answer.

6. What fraction of the map is purple and green? _____

   _____

7. What fraction of the map is red and blue? _____

   _____

8. What fraction of the map is blue and purple? _____

   _____

9. What fraction of the map is more green than yellow? _____

   _____

10. What fraction of the map is more red than blue? _____

   _____

11. What fraction of the map is more purple than red? _____

   _____

Unit 2: Adding and Subtracting Fractions—Adding and Subtracting Fractions With Like Denominators (cont.)

Show Your EXPERTISE!

Map of Counties in Oregon

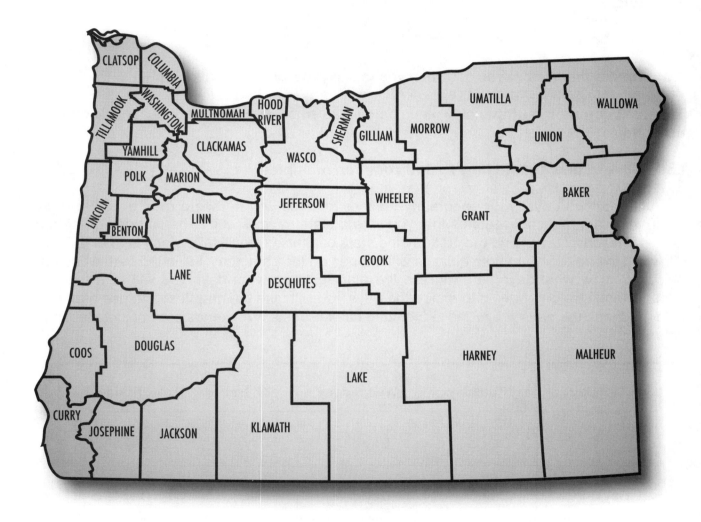

Unit 2: Adding and Subtracting Fractions— Finding Common Multiples

Let's EXPLORE!

Materials:
❑ Crayons

Vocabulary:
↳ multiple
↳ least common multiple

A **multiple** is the number you get when you multiply two or more other numbers.

The **least common multiple** of two numbers is the smallest number that is a multiple of both numbers.

Let's work to understand how to find common multiples.

Every two days, your geography teacher requires you to take a map quiz. Every five days, that same teacher requires that you take a state capitals quiz. The first day of the map quiz is Tuesday, Day 2, and the first day the state capitals quiz will take place is Friday, Day 5. We want to find out when both quizzes will happen on the same day. Fill in the partial calendar below to show what days you will take the map test and what days you will take the state capitals test. Use one crayon to shade the days you will take the map test and use a different color to shade the days you will take the state capitals tests. Weekends are not included in the calendar.

Monday	Tuesday	Wednesday	Thursday	Friday
Day 1	Day 2	Day 3	Day 4	Day 5
Day 6	Day 7	Day 8	Day 9	Day 10
Day 11	Day 12	Day 13	Day 14	Day 15
Day 16	Day 17	Day 18	Day 19	Day 20

Unit 2: Adding and Subtracting Fractions— Finding Common Multiples (cont.)

1. On what days did you take the map quiz? _____
    _____

2. On what days did you take the state capitals quiz? _____
    _____

3. On what days did you take both quizzes? _____
    _____

4. List the first 10 multiples of 2. _____

5. What do the multiples of two have in common with the days you took the map quiz? Use complete sentences in your answer. _____
    _____
    _____

6. List the first 10 multiples of 5. _____

7. What do the multiples of five have in common with the days you took the state capitals quiz? Use complete sentences in your answer. _____
    _____
    _____

8. What are the common multiples of 2 and 5? _____

9. What is the least common multiple of 2 and 5? _____

10. What does the least common multiple have in common with the days that both quizzes were taken? Use complete sentences in your answer. _____
    _____
    _____

Let's map out the answer to the question below to wrap up our exploration!

11. Will listing multiples of numbers work every time for finding common multiples? Why? Use complete sentences in your answer. _____
    _____
    _____

Name: _____ Date: _____

Unit 2: Adding and Subtracting Fractions— Finding Common Multiples (cont.)

Let's EXERCISE!

Listing Multiples

List the first 8 multiples of each number.

1. 3 _____   *2.* 4 _____

3. 10 _____   *4.* 12 _____

5. 2 _____   *6.* 9 _____

Finding Common Multiples

Find the least common multiple of the numbers.

7. 3, 12   *8.* 7, 10   *9.* 9, 21

_____   _____   _____

10. 6, 9, 10   *11.* 2, 4, 7   *12.* 4, 10, 25

_____   _____   _____

Find two common multiples of the numbers.

13. 5, 8   *14.* 3, 11

_____   _____

Extend Your Knowledge!

15. What would the least common multiple be of two numbers if one of them is 1? Why? Use complete sentences in your answer.

_____

_____

_____

28

Name: _____ Date: _____

Unit 2: Adding and Subtracting Fractions— Finding Common Multiples (cont.)

Show Your EXPERTISE!

Using Schedules to Find Common Multiples

You have three pets—a bird, a snake, and a dog. You feed the bird every two days, the snake every 6 days and the dog every day. Make a one-month, 31-day calendar of the feeding schedule for your pets. Use the calendar to answer the following questions.

1. What days do you feed both your bird and snake? _____

_____

2. What is the least common multiple of the number of days you must feed your bird and

snake? _____

3. What days do you feed both your snake and dog? _____

_____

4. What is the least common multiple of the number of days you must feed your snake and

dog? _____

5. What days must you feed all three animals? _____

_____

6. What is the least common multiple of the number of days you must feed all your animals?

_____

7. What animal is fed on days where the other two are always being fed as well?

_____

8. You receive a lizard for your birthday that needs to be fed every 5 days. Without using the

calendar, what day or days in the month would you need to feed all your animals?

_____

Name: _____ Date: _____

Unit 2: Adding and Subtracting Fractions—Adding and Subtracting Fractions With Unlike Denominators

Let's EXPLORE!

Materials:
- ❑ Outline of flag
- ❑ Purple and orange crayons

Vocabulary:
- 👆 least common denominator

The **least common denominator** is the smallest multiple that all denominators can be changed into using multiplication.

Let's flag down adding with unlike denominators!

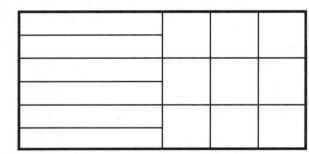

> ➢ Each stripe on the flag is $\frac{1}{12}$ of the flag.

> ➢ Each square on the flag is $\frac{1}{18}$ of the flag.

1. Color 2 of the stripes purple and 4 of the stripes orange. Color 2 of the squares orange and 7 of the squares purple.

2. If each stripe on the flag represents $\frac{1}{12}$ of the flag, how much of the flag are purple stripes?

$$\frac{\text{number of purple stripes}}{12} = \frac{\boxed{}}{12}$$

3. If each square on the flag is $\frac{1}{18}$ of the flag, how much of the flag are purple squares?

$$\frac{\text{number of purple squares}}{18} = \frac{\boxed{}}{18}$$

4. What operation would we have to identify in order to find out how much of the flag is

purple? _____

Unit 2: Adding and Subtracting Fractions—Adding and Subtracting Fractions With Unlike Denominators (cont.)

5. In order to perform the operation from Question 4, we need to find a common denominator for the fractions from Questions 2 and 3. What is the least common multiple both denominators can be changed into?

_____

6. What must you multiply 12 by to get the common denominator? _____

7. Use your answer from Question 2.

$$\frac{\boxed{}}{12} \quad \text{x} \quad \frac{\text{answer from Question 6}\;\boxed{}}{\text{answer from Question 6}\;\boxed{}} = \frac{\boxed{}}{\boxed{}}$$

8. What must you multiply 18 by to get the common denominator? _____

9. Use your answer from Question 8 to rewrite the fraction from Question 3.

$$\frac{\boxed{}}{18} \quad \text{x} \quad \frac{\text{answer from Question 8}\;\boxed{}}{\text{answer from Question 8}\;\boxed{}} = \frac{\boxed{}}{\boxed{}}$$

10. Use the fractions from Questions 7 and 9 to perform the operation from Question 4 to find the total of the flag that is purple.

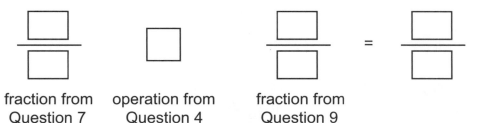

fraction from   operation from   fraction from
Question 7   Question 4   Question 9

11. Simplify the fraction from Question 10. _____

Name: _____   Date: _____

Unit 2: Adding and Subtracting Fractions–Adding and Subtracting Fractions With Unlike Denominators (cont.)

When we subtract fractions with unlike denominators, the same steps from above are used. The only difference is the operation performed on the numerators.

12. Use the fractions we found from Questions 7 and 9 to find how much more of the flag is purple squares than purple stripes. Simplify the answer.

$$\frac{\boxed{}}{\boxed{}} - \frac{\boxed{}}{\boxed{}} = \frac{\boxed{}}{\boxed{}} = \frac{\boxed{}}{\boxed{}}$$

fraction from   fraction from   simplified
Question 9   Question 7   answer

Name: _____ Date: _____

Unit 2: Adding and Subtracting Fractions—Adding and Subtracting Fractions With Unlike Denominators (cont.)

Let's EXERCISE!

Adding Fractions

Write the fraction represented by the picture, and then add the fractions by finding a common denominator to rewrite the fractions. Simplify your answer when necessary.

1.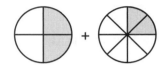

2.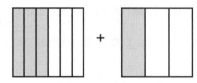

_____ + _____ = _____   _____ + _____ = _____

Add the fractions by rewriting the problem so the fractions have common denominators. Simplify your answer when necessary.

3. $\frac{2}{9} + \frac{5}{18}$ = _____   **4.** $\frac{1}{6} + \frac{2}{8}$ = _____

Subtracting Fractions

Write the fraction represented by the picture, and then subtract the fractions by rewriting them with a common denominator. Simplify your answer when necessary.

5.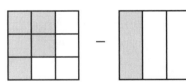

6.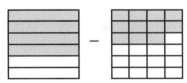

_____ − _____ = _____   _____ − _____ = _____

Subtract the fractions by rewriting the problem so the fractions have common denominators. Simplify your answer when necessary.

7. $\frac{9}{14} - \frac{3}{7}$ = _____   **8.** $\frac{5}{6} - \frac{3}{4}$ = _____

Extend Your Knowledge!

9. What would the least common denominator be when the numbers do not share any factors other than 1? Use complete sentences in your answer.

_____

_____

Unit 2: Adding and Subtracting Fractions—Adding and Subtracting Fractions With Unlike Denominators (cont.)

Show Your EXPERTISE!

Create a flag of your own using the nine squares and three rectangles on the next page to make your own flag. Each square is $\frac{1}{18}$ of your flag and each rectangle is $\frac{1}{6}$ of your flag. Your flag needs to be two different colors. Each color needs to be represented in the squares and rectangles. Glue your flag to a piece of paper and use it to answer the following questions.

1. How much of the first color is your flag? Write out the fractions and operation needed to answer this question. Simplify your answer.

   _____

   _____

2. How much of the second color is your flag? Write out the fractions and operation needed to answer this question. Simplify your answer.

   _____

   _____

3. How much more is the greater color than the lesser color of your flag? Write out the fractions and operation needed to answer this question. Simplify your answer.

   _____

   _____

4. How much more of the flag is the greater color squares than the lesser color rectangles? Write out the fractions and operation needed to answer this question. Simplify your answer.

   _____

   _____

Unit 2: Adding and Subtracting Fractions—Adding and Subtracting Fractions With Unlike Denominators (cont.)

Show Your EXPERTISE!

<u>**Shapes for creating your own flag**</u>

Unit 3: Mixed Numbers

Teacher Notes

Adding and Subtracting Mixed Numbers With Like Denominators

Let's EXPLORE!

Make a copy of the beehive frame page on a transparency. Cut each frame out and use them as overhead manipulatives. This will allow you to do the activity together as a class or to answer questions students may have as they are working.

Show Your EXPERTISE!

It is relatively simple to find images of the insects listed in this activity on the Internet. You could create a page with images that have the same measurements as those given in the activity. Then, the students could cut the images out to check their answer to Question 2. They could also try multiple arrangements of the insects and determine the range of widths for the styrofoam.

Adding and Subtracting Mixed Numbers With Unlike Denominators

Let's EXPLORE!

Make a copy of the acreage page on a transparency. Cut each acre out and use them as overhead manipulatives. This will allow you to do the activity together as a class or to answer questions students may have as they are working.

Name: _____ Date: _____

Unit 3: Mixed Numbers—Adding and Subtracting Mixed Numbers With Like Denominators

Let's EXPLORE!

Materials:
- ❑ Colored pencils
- ❑ Scissors
- ❑ One copy of beehive frame page
- ❑ Glue

Vocabulary:
- 🖐 mixed number

A **mixed number** consists of a whole number and a fraction, such as $2\frac{3}{4}$.

Making honey is a very complex process. Honeybees collect nectar, convert it to honey, and store it in their hives. Beekeepers build beehives to house bee colonies. These beehives are a set of wooden boxes without tops or bottoms. The wooden boxes are stacked on top of one another. Inside these boxes, several frames are hung parallel to one another. Bees build wax honeycombs in these frames to store the honey.

You are going to be a beekeeper in this Exploration.

1. You pull three frames out of your beehive. You discover that 2 of the frames are completely full of honey. Only 1 section of the third frame is full of honey. In the first row of your beehive frame paper, color the first 2 frames completely to show that they are full of honey. Color 1 section of the third frame to show that section is full of honey.

2. What fraction of the third frame is filled with honey? _____

3. Write a mixed number to represent how much of the three frames is filled with honey.

_____

4. You pull three more frames out of your beehive. You discover that 2 of the frames are completely full of honey. Only 2 sections of the third frame are full of honey. In the second row of your beehive frame paper, color the first 2 frames completely to show that they are full of honey. Color 2 sections of the third frame to show that those sections are full of honey.

5. What fraction of the third frame is filled with honey? _____

6. Write a mixed number to represent how much of these three frames is filled with honey.

_____

Unit 3: Mixed Numbers—Adding and Subtracting Mixed Numbers With Like Denominators (cont.)

7. Cut out the frames that you have colored. Paste the completely colored frames in four of the boxes below. Cut the colored sections out of the partially colored frames and paste them in the fifth box below.

8. How many completely colored frames do you have? _____

9. How many sections are colored? _____

10. Write a mixed number to represent the number of frames filled with honey. _____

11. Now, use your answers to Questions 3, 6, and 10 to write an addition sentence to show the total number of frames that are full of honey.

_____ + _____ = _____

12. You pull three new frames out of the beehive. You discover that 2 of the frames are completely full of honey, and 4 sections of the third frame are full of honey. In the third row of your beehive frame paper, color the first 2 frames completely to show that they are full of honey. Color 4 sections of the third frame to show that those sections are full of honey.

13. What fraction of the third frame is filled with honey? _____

Name: _____ Date: _____

Unit 3: Mixed Numbers—Adding and Subtracting Mixed Numbers With Like Denominators (cont.)

14. Write a mixed number to represent how much of these three frames is filled with honey.

_____

15. Cut out the frames that you have colored. You decide to harvest the honey from $1\frac{3}{5}$ of those frames. So, place 1 of the completely colored frames in the first box below. Then, cut 3 of the colored sections out and place them in the second box below.

16. Place the remaining frame in the first box below, and the remaining sections in the second box below.

17. Use your answer to Question 16 to determine how much honey you have left in the frames.

_____

18. Now, use your answers to Question 14, the mixed number in Question 15 and your answer to Question 17 to write a subtraction sentence to show the number of frames that are left full of honey.

_____ − _____ = _____

Name: _____ Date: _____

Unit 3: Mixed Numbers—Adding and Subtracting Mixed Numbers With Like Denominators (cont.)

Beehive Frames

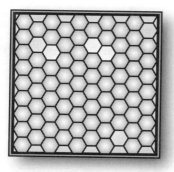 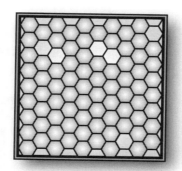 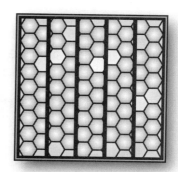

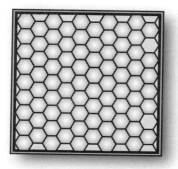 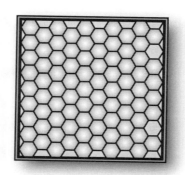 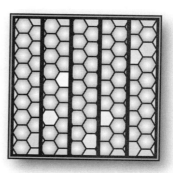

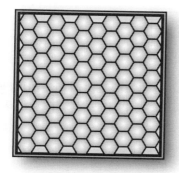 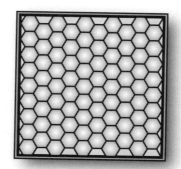 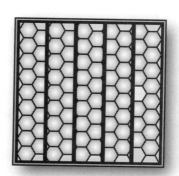

Unit 3: Mixed Numbers—Adding and Subtracting Mixed Numbers With Like Denominators (cont.)

Let's EXERCISE!

Use the diagrams to write addition and subtraction sentences below.

1. 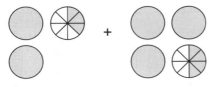 + 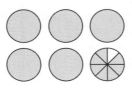 =

   _____ + _____ = _____

2. – =

   _____ – _____ = _____

Find the sum or difference. Write your answer in simplest form.

3. $1\frac{2}{5} + 3\frac{1}{5} =$ _____

4. $7\frac{7}{15} - 2\frac{4}{15} =$ _____

5. $4\frac{1}{8} + 2\frac{3}{8} =$ _____

6. $4\frac{4}{9} + 3\frac{2}{9} =$ _____

7. $5\frac{1}{3} + 1\frac{1}{3} =$ _____

8. $13\frac{9}{20} - 10\frac{7}{20} =$ _____

9. $7\frac{5}{6} - 6\frac{1}{6} =$ _____

10. $9\frac{5}{14} - 4\frac{3}{14} =$ _____

11. $3\frac{3}{10} + 5\frac{1}{10} =$ _____

12. $8\frac{1}{4} + 7\frac{1}{4} =$ _____

13. $2\frac{3}{7} - 1\frac{2}{7} =$ _____

14. $6\frac{7}{18} - 5\frac{5}{18} =$ _____

Name: _____ Date: _____

Unit 3: Mixed Numbers—Adding and Subtracting Mixed Numbers With Like Denominators (cont.)

Show Your EXPERTISE!

Your younger brother has asked you to help him prepare a display of his insect collection. The names and lengths of the insects in his collection are given in the table at right.

Insect	Length in Inches
Bumblebee	$1\frac{1}{16}$
Praying mantis	$2\frac{13}{16}$
Grasshopper	$1\frac{3}{16}$
Cockroach	$1\frac{7}{16}$
Dragonfly	$2\frac{9}{16}$
Cicada	$1\frac{11}{16}$

1. Your brother would like to place two insects beside each other so that he has three rows with two insects in each row. Decide which bugs will be placed beside each other and list them in the table below.

2. Use the lengths of the insects given to determine the minimum width of styrofoam needed to display the insects as you have them listed above. Show your work and write your answer in simplest form.

_____

_____

As part of the project, your brother must compare the lengths of the insects.

3. How much longer is the praying mantis than the bumblebee? Show your work and write your answer in simplest form.

_____

4. How much longer is the dragonfly than the cockroach? Show your work and write your answer in simplest form.

_____

Name: _____ Date: _____

Unit 3: Mixed Numbers—Adding and Subtracting Mixed Numbers With Unlike Denominators

Let's EXPLORE!

Materials:
- ❏ Yellow, orange, green, and red colored pencils, markers, or crayons
- ❏ Acreage page
- ❏ Scissors
- ❏ Glue

In this Exploration, you are going to be a farmer. You will need to plan how you are going to plant your fields. This year you plan to plant corn, pumpkins, and tomatoes.

1. You decide to plant $2\frac{1}{4}$ acres of corn. In the first row of your acreage page, color the first 2 acres and $\frac{1}{4}$ of the last acre in the row yellow.

2. You decide to plant $2\frac{5}{8}$ acres of pumpkins. In the second row of your acreage page, color the first 2 acres and $\frac{5}{8}$ of the last acre in the row orange.

3. You decide to plant $1\frac{11}{16}$ acres of tomatoes. In the third row of your acreage page, color the first acre and $\frac{11}{16}$ of the last acre in the row red.

4. You want to determine how many acres of corn and tomatoes you have planted. Cut out the acres in which you have planted corn and tomatoes. Glue them in the space below.

Name: _____ Date: _____

Unit 3: Mixed Numbers—Adding and Subtracting Mixed Numbers With Unlike Denominators (cont.)

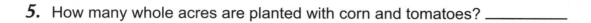

5. How many whole acres are planted with corn and tomatoes? _____

6. Cut out the $\frac{1}{4}$ acre of corn. Lay it on top of the acre that is divided into sixteenths below.

How many sixteenths is it equivalent to? _____

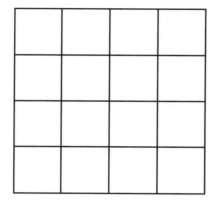

7. How many sixteenths of corn and tomatoes are there? _____

8. Use your answers to Questions 5 and 7 to determine how many total acres of corn and tomatoes you planted.

_____

9. Complete the addition sentence below to show how many acres of corn and tomatoes you planted.

_____ + _____ = _____

Name: _____   Date: _____

Unit 3: Mixed Numbers—Adding and Subtracting Mixed Numbers With Unlike Denominators (cont.)

10. You want to determine how many more whole acres of pumpkins than corn you planted. Cut out the whole acres in which you have planted pumpkins and glue them in the open space below. Then shade the two acres below it with yellow to indicate the number of whole acres of corn you planted.

11. How many more whole acres of pumpkins than corn have you planted? _____

12. Lay the $\frac{1}{4}$ acre of corn on top of the acre that has been divided into eighths at right. How many eighths is it equivalent to?

_____

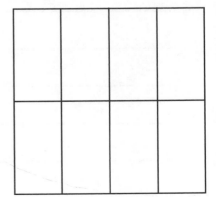

Unit 3: Mixed Numbers—Adding and Subtracting Mixed Numbers With Unlike Denominators (cont.)

13. How many more eighths of pumpkins than corn did you plant? _____

14. Use your answers to Questions 11 and 13 to determine how many more acres of pumpkins than corn you planted.

_____

15. Complete the subtraction sentence below to show how many more acres of pumpkins than corn you planted.

_____ – _____ = _____

16. What did you do in Questions 6 and 12 that helped you add and subtract mixed numbers with unlike denominators? Use complete sentences in your answer.

_____

_____

_____

_____

17. How does the process for adding and subtracting mixed numbers with unlike denominators differ from the process for adding and subtracting mixed numbers with like denominators? Use complete sentences in your answer.

_____

_____

_____

_____

_____

Name: _____ Date: _____

Acreage Page

Row 1

Row 2

Row 3

Name: _____ Date: _____

Unit 3: Mixed Numbers—Adding and Subtracting Mixed Numbers With Unlike Denominators (cont.)

Let's EXERCISE!

Use the diagrams to write addition and subtraction sentences below.

1.    +   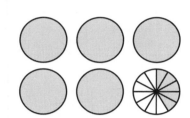   =

_____   +   _____   =   _____

2. 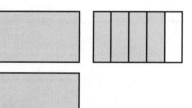   –   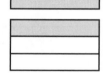   =

_____   –   _____   =   _____

Find the sum or difference. Write your answer in simplest form.

3. $2\frac{3}{5} + 4\frac{3}{10} =$ _____

4. $5\frac{7}{8} - 3\frac{3}{4} =$ _____

5. $7\frac{14}{15} - 3\frac{7}{10} =$ _____

6. $9\frac{4}{7} + 3\frac{8}{21} =$ _____

7. $1\frac{1}{9} + 2\frac{5}{12} =$ _____

8. $10\frac{2}{5} - 8\frac{1}{6} =$ _____

9. $8\frac{3}{4} - 5\frac{1}{3} =$ _____

10. $7\frac{8}{9} - 2\frac{5}{6} =$ _____

11. $4\frac{1}{6} + 3\frac{3}{8} =$ _____

12. $6\frac{5}{12} + 1\frac{4}{15} =$ _____

13. $9\frac{11}{12} - 6\frac{3}{8} =$ _____

14. $5\frac{3}{16} + 4\frac{7}{24} =$ _____

Name: _____ Date: _____

Unit 3: Mixed Numbers—Adding and Subtracting Mixed Numbers With Unlike Denominators (cont.)

Show Your EXPERTISE!

You pick five pumpkins from your pumpkin patch and weigh them. Their weights are recorded in the table below. Use the weights to answer the questions.

Pumpkin 1	$10\frac{1}{3}$ pounds
Pumpkin 2	$9\frac{2}{3}$ pounds
Pumpkin 3	$9\frac{1}{5}$ pounds
Pumpkin 4	$9\frac{1}{4}$ pounds
Pumpkin 5	$10\frac{3}{8}$ pounds

You are going to sell your pumpkins at the farmers' market. The price of a pumpkin is based on how much it weighs. The bigger the pumpkin, the more it costs.

1. A customer wants to buy two pumpkins. Which two pumpkins should she buy to spend the least? What would be their total weight? Show your work and write your answer in simplest form.

   _____

2. Which two pumpkins should she buy if she wants the biggest pumpkins? What would be their total weight? Show your work and write your answer in simplest form.

   _____

3. A customer would like to know the range of size of your pumpkins. That is, he would like to know how much bigger the largest pumpkin is than the smallest pumpkin. What will you tell him? Show your work and write your answer in simplest form.

   _____

4. After looking your pumpkins over, he argues that the range of size of your pumpkins is $1\frac{2}{3}$. What mistake did he make in calculating the range in size?

   _____

   _____

Unit 4: Mixed Numbers and Improper Fractions

Teacher Notes

Mixed Numbers and Improper Fractions

Let's EXPLORE!

You could use dry beans for this Exploration instead of rice. You could also do this Exploration as a class or put the students in groups if you do not have enough measuring cups and other materials for individual students. To help the activity run smoothly, it is a good idea to have the rice measured out and labeled prior to the class time in which you would like to do this activity. It is also a good idea to provide each student or group with a bowl large enough to hold the rice. This will make cleanup easier.

Show Your EXPERTISE!

As an extension to this activity, you could ask the class to come to a consensus about the measurements and then mix the ingredients per their suggestions in class. Bake the biscuits at home and bring them in for the students to try.

Adding Mixed Numbers With Regrouping

Let's EXPLORE!

You could use dry beans for this Exploration instead of rice. You could also do this Exploration as a class or put the students in groups if you do not have enough measuring cups and other materials for individual students. To help the activity run smoothly, make sure that each student or group of students has enough rice in the bag to complete the Exploration. It is a good idea to provide each student or group with a bowl large enough to hold the rice. This will make cleanup easier.

Subtracting Mixed Numbers With Regrouping

Let's EXPLORE!

You could use dry beans for this Exploration instead of rice. You could also do this Exploration as a class or put the students in groups if you do not have enough measuring cups and other materials for individual students. To help the activity run smoothly, make sure that each student or group of students has enough rice in the bag to complete the Exploration. It is a good idea to provide each student or group with a bowl large enough to hold the rice. This will make cleanup easier.

Show Your EXPERTISE!

As an extension to this activity, have students make gak, putty, and/or slime. You may choose to have the students add food coloring to customize their creations.

Name: _____   Date: _____

Unit 4: Mixed Numbers and Improper Fractions

Let's EXPLORE!

Materials:
- ❑ Measuring cups
- ❑ Bags of rice
- ❑ Bowls

Vocabulary:
- ✍ improper fraction

An **improper fraction** is a fraction in which the numerator is greater than the denominator.

We can write improper fractions as mixed numbers and mixed numbers as improper fractions. But how?

Let's explore and find out!

1. Your teacher will give you a bag labeled $\frac{8}{4}$, because it has $\frac{8}{4}$ cups of rice in it.

2. Use your $\frac{1}{4}$-cup measuring cup to verify that your bag has $\frac{8}{4}$ cups of rice in it.

3. Use your 1-cup measuring cup to determine how many whole cups are in $\frac{8}{4}$ cups of rice.

    How many whole cups are there? _____

4. Use a complete sentence to describe the relationship between $\frac{8}{4}$ and your answer to Question 3.

    _____

    _____

5. Your teacher will give you a bag labeled $\frac{10}{4}$, because it has $\frac{10}{4}$ cups of rice in it.

6. Use your $\frac{1}{4}$-cup measuring cup to verify that your bag has $\frac{10}{4}$ cups of rice in it.

7. Use your 1-cup measuring cup to determine how many cups are in $\frac{10}{4}$ cups of rice.

    How many whole cups are there? _____

8. How many fourths are left over? $\dfrac{\boxed{}}{4}$

Unit 4: Mixed Numbers and Improper Fractions (cont.)

9. Use a complete sentence to describe the relationship between $\frac{10}{4}$ and your answers to Questions 7 and 8.

_____

_____

10. Write the improper fraction $\frac{10}{4}$ as a mixed number. (Hint: Use your answers to Questions 7 and 8.) _____

11. The fraction bar in a fraction indicates division. So, $\frac{8}{4}$ means $8 \div 4$ and $\frac{10}{4}$ means $10 \div 4$. Use this information to help you explain how to write an improper fraction as a mixed number.

_____

_____

_____

12. Your teacher will give you a bag of rice labeled 2 cups. Use your 1-cup measuring cup to verify that you have that much rice in your bag.

13. Use your $\frac{1}{3}$-cup measuring cup to determine the number of thirds of rice you have.

_____

14. Write your answer to Question 13 over 3 to show how many thirds are in 2 cups of rice.

_____

15. Use a complete sentence to describe the relationship between 2 and your answer to Question 14. _____

_____

_____

Unit 4: Mixed Numbers and Improper Fractions (cont.)

16. Your teacher will give you a bag of rice labeled $2\frac{2}{3}$ cups. Use your 1-cup and $\frac{1}{3}$-cup measuring cups to verify that you have that much rice in your bag.

17. Use your $\frac{1}{3}$-cup measuring cup to determine the number of thirds of rice you have.

_____

18. Write your answer to Question 17 over 3 to show how many thirds are in $2\frac{2}{3}$ cups of rice.

_____

19. Use a complete sentence to describe the relationship between $2\frac{2}{3}$ and your answer to Question 18. _____

_____

_____

20. If you divide to write an improper fraction as a mixed number, what operation do you think you will use to write a mixed number as an improper fraction? _____

21. To write a mixed number as an improper fraction, you must also use addition. The diagram at right shows what you should do. Use the diagram and what you have learned on this exploration to explain how to write a mixed number as an improper fraction.

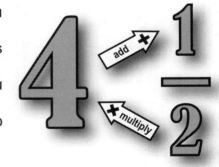

_____

_____

_____

Unit 4: Mixed Numbers and Improper Fractions (cont.)

Let's EXERCISE!

Write the improper fractions as mixed numbers. Write your answers in simplest form.

1. $\dfrac{15}{8}$ = _____

2. $\dfrac{20}{6}$ = _____

3. $\dfrac{25}{7}$ = _____

4. $\dfrac{32}{9}$ = _____

5. $\dfrac{18}{5}$ = _____

6. $\dfrac{20}{3}$ = _____

7. $\dfrac{46}{8}$ = _____

8. $\dfrac{17}{2}$ = _____

9. $\dfrac{38}{4}$ = _____

10. $\dfrac{43}{10}$ = _____

Write the mixed numbers as improper fractions.

11. $2\dfrac{1}{5}$ = _____

12. $3\dfrac{5}{7}$ = _____

13. $1\dfrac{8}{9}$ = _____

14. $2\dfrac{5}{6}$ = _____

15. $3\dfrac{1}{4}$ = _____

16. $4\dfrac{3}{8}$ = _____

17. $1\dfrac{7}{10}$ = _____

18. $2\dfrac{3}{10}$ = _____

19. $5\dfrac{1}{2}$ = _____

20. $4\dfrac{3}{5}$ = _____

Unit 4: Mixed Numbers and Improper Fractions (cont.)

Show Your EXPERTISE!

1. You are making cheese biscuits for your class bake sale. You cannot find the 1-cup measuring cup or the 1-teaspoon measuring spoon. You decide to rewrite the measurements as improper fractions so that you can use the fractional measuring cups and spoons. Complete the improper fraction column in the ingredients table.

Amount	Ingredient	Improper Fraction
$3\frac{3}{4}$ cups	all-purpose flour	
$4\frac{1}{2}$ teaspoons	baking powder	
$1\frac{1}{8}$ teaspoons	salt	
$\frac{1}{2}$ teaspoon	baking soda	
$\frac{1}{2}$ cup	shortening	
$2\frac{1}{4}$ cups	shredded cheddar cheese	
$1\frac{3}{4}$ cups	buttermilk	

2. You are also making garlic bread for the bake sale. Your grandmother tells you that you will need $\frac{4}{3}$ cups of butter to make four loaves. Your grandmother asks you to help her figure out how many cups of butter you will need. Write the amount of butter needed for four loaves as a mixed number. Then use complete sentences to explain what you did.

_____

_____

_____

Name: _____   Date: _____

Unit 4: Mixed Numbers and Improper Fractions– Adding Mixed Numbers With Regrouping

Let's EXPLORE!

Materials:
- ❑ Measuring cups
- ❑ Bags of rice
- ❑ Bowls

Vocabulary:
- ↬ regroup

Sometimes when you add mixed numbers, you end up with a mixed number that contains an improper fraction, like $3\frac{7}{5}$. It is not good mathematical form to leave the number this way, so you must **regroup**. You need to change the improper fraction $\frac{7}{5}$ to the mixed number $1\frac{2}{5}$ and add the whole number to the 3 to get $4\frac{2}{5}$.

Let's explore with measuring cups to help us develop good mathematical form when adding mixed numbers!

1. Use your measuring cups to measure out $1\frac{2}{3}$ cups of rice.

2. Now, measure out $2\frac{2}{3}$ cups of rice and add it to the rice that you already have.

3. Use your 1-cup and $\frac{1}{3}$-cup measuring cups to measure the rice. How many whole cups do you have? _____

4. How many thirds do you have? _____

5. Use your answers to Questions 3 and 4 to write a mixed number that represents the total amount of rice you have. _____

6. Add $1\frac{2}{3}$ and $2\frac{2}{3}$. What is the sum? _____

7. Rewrite the improper fraction in your answer to Question 6 as a mixed number. _____

8. Add the whole number from Question 6 to your answer to Question 7. _____

56

Unit 4: Mixed Numbers and Improper Fractions— Adding Mixed Numbers With Regrouping (cont.)

9. Use a complete sentence to explain how your answer to Question 8 compares to your answer to Question 5. _____

_____

10. Use your measuring cups to measure out $1\frac{3}{4}$ cups of rice.

11. Now, measure out $2\frac{2}{4}$ cups of rice and add it to the rice that you already have.

12. Use your 1-cup and $\frac{1}{4}$-cup measuring cups to measure the rice. How many whole cups do you have? _____

13. How many fourths do you have? _____

14. Use your answers to Questions 12 and 13 to write a mixed number that represents the total amount of rice you have. _____

15. Add $1\frac{3}{4}$ and $2\frac{2}{4}$. What is the sum? _____

16. Rewrite the improper fraction in your answer to Question 15 as a mixed number. _____

17. Add the whole number from Question 15 to your answer to Question 16. _____

18. Use a complete sentence to explain how your answer to Question 17 compares to your answer to Question 14. _____

_____

19. Use a complete sentence to explain when you need to use regrouping when adding mixed numbers. _____

_____

20. Explain how you would use regrouping to find the sum of $2\frac{3}{8}$ and $4\frac{7}{8}$.

_____

_____

_____

Name: _____ Date: _____

Unit 4: Mixed Numbers and Improper Fractions— Adding Mixed Numbers With Regrouping (cont.)

Let's EXERCISE!

Find the sum. Write your answer in simplest form.

1. $2\frac{3}{7} + 4\frac{6}{7} =$ _____

2. $3\frac{3}{5} + 1\frac{4}{5} =$ _____

3. $5\frac{7}{8} + 2\frac{5}{8} =$ _____

4. $4\frac{5}{9} + 6\frac{7}{9} =$ _____

5. $8\frac{5}{6} + 1\frac{5}{6} =$ _____

6. $3\frac{13}{15} + 5\frac{11}{15} =$ _____

7. $2\frac{9}{10} + 7\frac{7}{10} =$ _____

8. $5\frac{4}{5} + 1\frac{2}{5} =$ _____

9. $3\frac{7}{12} + 6\frac{11}{12} =$ _____

10. $8\frac{5}{16} + 4\frac{15}{16} =$ _____

11. $2\frac{1}{2} + 3\frac{3}{4} =$ _____

12. $6\frac{2}{3} + 8\frac{5}{6} =$ _____

13. $4\frac{5}{8} + 5\frac{7}{12} =$ _____

14. $2\frac{5}{9} + 9\frac{7}{12} =$ _____

15. $6\frac{5}{7} + 1\frac{9}{14} =$ _____

16. $8\frac{4}{5} + 5\frac{2}{3} =$ _____

17. $9\frac{9}{10} + 10\frac{3}{5} =$ _____

18. $7\frac{9}{15} + 5\frac{11}{12} =$ _____

19. $8\frac{7}{9} + 7\frac{5}{6} =$ _____

20. $4\frac{6}{7} + 8\frac{2}{3} =$ _____

Unit 4: Mixed Numbers and Improper Fractions— Adding Mixed Numbers With Regrouping (cont.)

Show Your EXPERTISE!

Below are lists of the ingredients and amounts needed to make loaves of three different types of bread. Find the total amount of the ingredients listed in the table that you would need to make all three of the recipes. Show your work on another piece of paper. Then fill in the table with your answers in simplest form.

Honey French Bread

- $3\frac{3}{4}$ cups water
- 10 teaspoons honey
- 10 teaspoons olive oil
- $3\frac{1}{3}$ teaspoons salt
- $3\frac{1}{3}$ teaspoons white sugar
- 10 cups bread flour
- $7\frac{1}{7}$ teaspoons active dry yeast

Oatmeal Bread

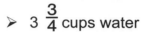
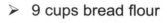

- $3\frac{3}{4}$ cups water
- 9 cups bread flour
- 6 tablespoons honey
- $4\frac{1}{2}$ tablespoons dry milk powder
- $4\frac{1}{2}$ teaspoons salt
- $1\frac{1}{2}$ cups quick cooking oats
- 6 tablespoons margarine
- 9 teaspoons active dry yeast

Cracked Wheat Bread

- $2\frac{1}{2}$ cups water
- 4 tablespoons margarine
- 4 tablespoons dry milk powder
- 4 tablespoons brown sugar
- $2\frac{1}{2}$ teaspoons salt
- 6 cups bread flour
- $\frac{2}{3}$ cup whole wheat flour
- $\frac{1}{2}$ cup cracked wheat
- $2\frac{1}{2}$ teaspoons active dry yeast

Ingredient	Amount
Water	
Honey	
Salt	
Bread flour	
Active dry yeast	
Margarine	
Dry milk powder	

Name: _____ Date: _____

Unit 4: Mixed Numbers and Improper Fractions— Subtracting Mixed Numbers With Regrouping

Let's EXPLORE!

Materials:
- ❑ Measuring cups
- ❑ Bags of rice
- ❑ Bowls

Vocabulary:
- ✎ regrouping

Let's say your teacher asks you to find the following difference: $8\frac{1}{4} - 3\frac{3}{4} = ?$

You know that you should subtract the whole numbers and then the fractional parts of the mixed numbers. But, how can you subtract $\frac{3}{4}$ from $\frac{1}{4}$? You can use **regrouping** to help you solve this dilemma!

Let's explore with measuring cups to help us understand.

1. Use your measuring cups to measure out $3\frac{1}{4}$ cups of rice in a separate bowl.

2. Now, use your measuring cups to remove $1\frac{3}{4}$ cups of rice from the bowl containing $3\frac{1}{4}$ cups of rice.

3. Use your 1-cup and $\frac{1}{4}$-cup measuring cups to measure the rice that is left in the bowl. How many whole cups do you have? _____

4. How many fourths do you have? _____

5. Use your answers to Questions 3 and 4 to write a mixed number that represents the total amount of rice you have. _____

6. Are you surprised by your answer to Question 5? How many whole cups did you expect to have left? Use a complete sentence in your answer. _____

_____

7. Now use your measuring cups to measure out $4\frac{1}{3}$ cups of rice into a separate bowl.

Unit 4: Mixed Numbers and Improper Fractions— Subtracting Mixed Numbers With Regrouping (cont.)

8. Use your measuring cups to remove $2\frac{2}{3}$ cups of rice from the bowl containing $4\frac{1}{3}$ cups of rice.

9. Use your 1-cup and $\frac{1}{3}$-cup measuring cups to measure the rice that is left in the bowl. How many whole cups do you have? _____

10. How many thirds do you have? _____

11. Use your answers to Questions 9 and 10 to write a mixed number that represents the total amount of rice you have. _____

12. Are you surprised by your answer to Question 11? How many whole cups did you expect to have left? Use a complete sentence in your answer. _____

_____

Let's take a closer look at what is happening mathematically.

We'll find the difference of $3\frac{1}{4}$ and $1\frac{3}{4}$.

13. How many $\frac{1}{4}$ cups are in 1 cup? Use your measuring cups if you need them to help you figure this out. _____

14. So, we can say that $1 = \dfrac{\boxed{}}{4}$.

15. Add $\frac{1}{4}$ and your answer to Number 14. _____

16. We must regroup $3\frac{1}{4}$. We borrow 1 from the 3 and rewrite it as fourths. This leaves a 2 as the whole number part. Then we add these fourths to the $\frac{1}{4}$. Use your answer to Number 15 to complete the following statement.

$$3\frac{1}{4} = 2\,\dfrac{\boxed{}}{4}$$

Unit 4: Mixed Numbers and Improper Fractions— Subtracting Mixed Numbers With Regrouping (cont.)

17. Now, you can subtract $1\frac{3}{4}$ from $3\frac{1}{4}$ by using your answer to Question 16. Complete the subtraction sentence below.

$$3\frac{1}{4} - 1\frac{3}{4} = 2\frac{\boxed{}}{4} - 1\frac{3}{4} = \underline{}$$

Now, we'll find the difference of $4\frac{1}{3}$ and $2\frac{2}{3}$.

18. How many $\frac{1}{3}$ cups are in 1 cup? Use your measuring cups if you need them to help you figure this out. _____

19. So, we can say that $1 = \dfrac{\boxed{}}{3}$.

20. Add $\frac{1}{3}$ and your answer to Number 19. _____

21. We must regroup $4\frac{1}{3}$. We borrow 1 from the 4 and rewrite it as thirds. This leaves a 3 as the whole number part. Then we add these thirds to the $\frac{1}{3}$. Use your answer to Number 20 to complete the following statement.

$$4\frac{1}{3} = 3\frac{\boxed{}}{3}$$

22. Now, you can subtract $2\frac{2}{3}$ from $4\frac{1}{3}$ by using your answer to Question 21. Complete the subtraction sentence below.

$$4\frac{1}{3} - 2\frac{2}{3} = 3\frac{\boxed{}}{3} - 2\frac{2}{3} = \underline{}$$

Unit 4: Mixed Numbers and Improper Fractions— Subtracting Mixed Numbers With Regrouping (cont.)

Let's EXERCISE!

Regroup in each of the mixed numbers below. An example has been done for you.

Example: $5\frac{2}{5} = 4\frac{7}{5}$

1. $6\frac{1}{8} =$ _____

2. $7\frac{2}{9} =$ _____

3. $2\frac{1}{6} =$ _____

4. $9\frac{3}{7} =$ _____

Find the difference. Write your answer in simplest form.

5. $4\frac{1}{8} - 2\frac{3}{8} =$ _____

6. $8\frac{2}{7} - 3\frac{5}{7} =$ _____

7. $10\frac{1}{5} - 6\frac{4}{5} =$ _____

8. $9\frac{1}{6} - 1\frac{5}{6} =$ _____

9. $5\frac{2}{9} - 3\frac{7}{9} =$ _____

10. $6\frac{3}{8} - 4\frac{7}{8} =$ _____

11. $8\frac{5}{12} - 7\frac{11}{12} =$ _____

12. $12\frac{3}{10} - 5\frac{9}{10} =$ _____

13. $14\frac{1}{4} - 3\frac{3}{8} =$ _____

14. $10\frac{1}{3} - 2\frac{5}{9} =$ _____

15. $7\frac{1}{6} - 5\frac{3}{4} =$ _____

16. $6\frac{1}{4} - 1\frac{1}{3} =$ _____

17. $15\frac{1}{8} - 10\frac{5}{6} =$ _____

18. $7\frac{1}{5} - 2\frac{7}{10} =$ _____

19. $9\frac{3}{7} - 4\frac{10}{21} =$ _____

20. $10\frac{1}{2} - 9\frac{7}{12} =$ _____

Unit 4: Mixed Numbers and Improper Fractions— Subtracting Mixed Numbers With Regrouping (cont.)

Show Your EXPERTISE!

Below are lists of ingredients needed to make homemade gak, putty, and slime. Use these recipes to answer the questions that follow.

GAK

Part 1:
- $\frac{1}{4}$ cups water
- $\frac{1}{2}$ cups white glue

Part 2:
- $\frac{1}{2}$ teaspoons Borax
- $\frac{1}{4}$ cup warm water

SLIME
- $1\frac{2}{3}$ cups white glue
- $\frac{5}{6}$ cups liquid starch

PUTTY
- $2\frac{7}{8}$ cups white glue
- $2\frac{7}{8}$ cups liquid starch

1. How much more white glue do you need to make putty than to make gak? Show your work and write your answer in simplest form.

_____

_____

2. How much more white glue do you need to make slime than to make gak? Show your work and write your answer in simplest form.

_____

_____

3. How much more starch do you need for putty than for slime? Show your work and write your answer in simplest form.

_____

_____

4. Your friend says the answer to Question 3 should be 2 cups. Use complete sentences to explain what mistake he made in calculating his answer.

_____

_____

Unit 5: Multiplying and Dividing Fractions and Mixed Numbers

Teacher Notes

Multiplying Fractions

Let's EXPLORE!

Many craft or discount stores will be willing to donate fabric and ribbon if you explain that you are a teacher doing a math activity for a local shelter. If you can get a local news station to cover the activity, the store might be more willing to donate items when they know they will get some publicity.

Students should contact their local animal shelter to see what type of blankets they will take. A visit to the shelter would be nice as well.

Whatever materials are donated, you should measure out how much fabric and ribbon are needed so it matches the Exploration. Remind students that there are 36 inches in a yard when they are measuring to cut the materials.

Poster board could be used to substitute for the fabric and masking tape for the ribbon as a paper-pencil alternative.

Dividing Fractions

Let's EXPLORE!

Poster board could be used to substitute for the fabric and masking tape for the ribbon as a paper-pencil alternative.

Multiplying Mixed Numbers

Let's EXPLORE!

Masking tape can be substituted for the crepe paper streamers as a paper-pencil alternative.

Dividing Mixed Numbers

Let's EXPLORE!

You could contact the local newspaper and ask for their "end-rolls."

Poster board could be used to substitute for the newspaper as a paper-pencil alternative.

Name: _____ Date: _____

Unit 5: Multiplying and Dividing Fractions and Mixed Numbers—Multiplying Fractions

Let's EXPLORE!

Materials:
- ❑ Spool of ribbon
- ❑ Bolt of fabric

Making blankets can be easy. Let's blanket this Exploration to cover multiplying fractions.

You are making blankets for a local animal shelter. You are using donated fabric and ribbon to make the blankets. You have $\frac{2}{5}$ of a spool of ribbon and $\frac{7}{8}$ of a bolt of fabric. Use the fractions to answer the questions.

1. If the spool originally had $\frac{5}{9}$ yard of ribbon on it, how much ribbon is on the spool?

A. First, write out the multiplication problem.

x

length of
original ribbon

amount
on spool

B. Second, multiply the numerators and denominators of the fractions.

  x   =

length of
original ribbon

amount
on spool

C. Third, simplify your answer.

  =

Unit 5: Multiplying and Dividing Fractions and Mixed Numbers—Multiplying Fractions (cont.)

2. If the bolt originally had $\frac{6}{7}$ yard of fabric on it, how much fabric is on the bolt?

A. First, write out the multiplication problem.

   x

length of   amount
original fabric   on bolt

B. Second, multiply the numerators and denominators of the fractions.

   x   =

length of   amount
original fabric   on bolt

C. Third, simplify your answer.

   =

Let's wrap up this exploration by answering this question.

3. What types of values are there for the product of two fractions? Use complete sentences in your answer.

_____

_____

_____

Name: _____ Date: _____

 Unit 5: Multiplying and Dividing Fractions and Mixed Numbers—Multiplying Fractions (cont.)

Let's EXERCISE!

Multiplying Fractions

Write the fractions represented by the picture and then multiply them. Write your answer in simplest form.

1.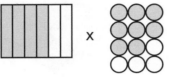

_____ x _____ = _____

2.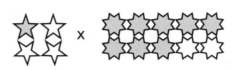

_____ x _____ = _____

Multiply the fractions. Write your answer in simplest form.

3. $\frac{3}{14} \times \frac{2}{11} =$ _____

4. $\frac{6}{13} \times \frac{1}{3} =$ _____

5. $\frac{5}{8} \times \frac{3}{4} =$ _____

6. $\frac{5}{7} \times \frac{5}{7} =$ _____

7. $\frac{2}{3} \times \frac{8}{15} \times \frac{1}{4} =$ _____

8. $\frac{5}{6} \times \frac{3}{5} \times \frac{2}{7} =$ _____

9. $\frac{4}{10} \times \frac{2}{9} =$ _____

10. $\frac{7}{8} \times \frac{1}{6} =$ _____

11. $\frac{14}{18} \times \frac{5}{25} =$ _____

12. $\frac{2}{3} \times \frac{8}{17} =$ _____

Extend Your Knowledge!

13. What is the product of a fraction and its reciprocal? _____

Name: _____ Date: _____

Unit 5: Multiplying and Dividing Fractions and Mixed Numbers—Multiplying Fractions (cont.)

Show Your EXPERTISE!

Multiplying Fractions

You are making blankets for a local homeless shelter. They need baby blankets. You are using donated fabric and ribbon to make the baby blankets. You have $\frac{2}{9}$ of a spool of red ribbon and $\frac{5}{7}$ of a spool of blue ribbon. There is $\frac{3}{4}$ of a bolt of pink fabric and $\frac{8}{9}$ of a bolt of yellow fabric. Use the fractions to answer the questions. Write your answers in simplest form.

1. If the spool of red ribbon originally had $\frac{7}{9}$ yard of ribbon, how much red ribbon is there?

_____ Write out the multiplication problem and show all the steps.

2. If the spool of blue ribbon originally had $\frac{5}{8}$ yard of ribbon, how much blue ribbon is there?

_____ Write out the multiplication problem and show all the steps.

3. If the bolt of pink fabric originally had $\frac{7}{12}$ yard of fabric, how much pink fabric is there?

_____ Write out the multiplication problem and show all the steps.

4. If the bolt of yellow fabric originally had $\frac{4}{5}$ yard of fabric, how much yellow fabric is there?

_____ Write out the multiplication problem and show all the steps.

Unit 5: Multiplying and Dividing Fractions and Mixed Numbers—Dividing Fractions

Let's EXPLORE!

Materials:
- ❑ Spool of ribbon
- ❑ Bolt of fabric
- ❑ Pinking shears

Divide and conquer this exploration to learn more about fractions!

You are making kitchen towels to sell at a fund-raiser for your class. You want to make as many kitchen towels as you possibly can out of donated fabric and ribbon. A fellow classmate has brought in $\frac{6}{7}$ yard of ribbon on a spool and $\frac{4}{5}$ yard of fabric on a bolt. Each kitchen towel should be as wide as the bolt of fabric and $\frac{1}{6}$-yard long so it can be folded in half. Each kitchen towel uses $\frac{1}{9}$ yard of ribbon. Use the fractions to answer the questions.

1. How many kitchen towels can be made from the fabric?

A. First, write out the division problem.

$$\frac{\boxed{}}{\boxed{}} \div \frac{\boxed{}}{\boxed{}}$$

length   fabric needed for
of fabric   each kitchen towel

B. Second, invert the second fraction, and then multiply the numerators and denominators.

$$\frac{\boxed{}}{\boxed{}} \quad \begin{matrix} \text{x} \\ \text{x} \end{matrix} \quad \frac{\boxed{}}{\boxed{}} = \frac{\boxed{}}{\boxed{}}$$

length   inverted amount of
of fabric   fabric needed for
           each kitchen towel

C. Third, simplify your fraction.

$$\frac{\boxed{}}{\boxed{}} = \boxed{} \frac{\boxed{}}{\boxed{}}$$

Unit 5: Multiplying and Dividing Fractions and Mixed Numbers—Dividing Fractions (cont.)

D. Because you can't make a fraction of a towel, your answer will be the whole number in the mixed number. Use your answer from part C to cut the whole number of kitchen towels out of the fabric using the pinking shears.

2. How many kitchen towels can be made with the spool of ribbon?

A. First, write out the division problem.

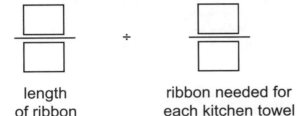

         length   ribbon needed for
         of ribbon   each kitchen towel

B. Second, invert the second fraction, and then multiply the numerators and denominators.

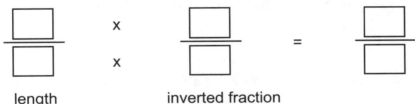

         length   inverted fraction
         of ribbon   of ribbon needed
                       for each kitchen towel

C. Third, simplify your answer.

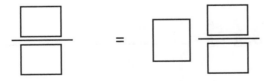

D. Use your answer from part C to cut up the whole number of ribbons for each kitchen towel.

Let's finish this exploration by answering this question.

3. Can you divide a smaller fraction by a larger fraction? Use complete sentences to explain

why or why not. _____

_____

_____

Name: _____ Date: _____

Unit 5: Multiplying and Dividing Fractions and Mixed Numbers—Dividing Fractions (cont.)

Let's EXERCISE!

Dividing Fractions

Write the fractions represented by the picture and then divide them. Write your answer as a mixed number when necessary. Write your answer in simplest form.

1.

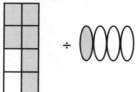

_____ ÷ _____

_____ x _____ = _____

2.

_____ ÷ _____

_____ x _____ = _____

Divide the fractions by inverting the second fraction and then changing to multiplication. Show all the steps. Write your answer as a mixed number when necessary. Write your answer in simplest form.

3. $\frac{3}{10} \div \frac{1}{5}$ = _____

4. $\frac{2}{7} \div \frac{5}{14}$ = _____

5. $\frac{4}{9} \div \frac{12}{13}$ = _____

6. $\frac{8}{11} \div \frac{2}{3}$ = _____

7. $\frac{13}{15} \div \frac{2}{5}$ = _____

8. $\frac{7}{8} \div \frac{5}{8}$ = _____

9. $\frac{5}{6} \div \frac{3}{4}$ = _____

10. $\frac{6}{10} \div \frac{1}{2}$ = _____

Extend Your Knowledge!

11. What is the quotient of a fraction and itself? _____

Unit 5: Multiplying and Dividing Fractions and Mixed Numbers—Dividing Fractions (cont.)

Show Your EXPERTISE!

Dividing Fractions

Your class is going to have a fund-raiser for a future class trip. For your fund-raiser, the class decides to make decorative Christmas bows. Your classmates have brought in 4 spools of ribbon. A green spool has $\frac{3}{4}$ yard of ribbon. A red spool has $\frac{2}{3}$ yard of ribbon. A white spool has $\frac{8}{9}$ yard of ribbon. A gold spool has $\frac{6}{7}$ yard of ribbon. Use the fractions to answer the questions. Write your answer in simplest form.

1. If you want to make green bows that are $\frac{3}{8}$-yard long, how many bows can you make with the green spool of ribbon? _____ Write out the division problem and show all the steps.

2. If you want to make red bows that are $\frac{1}{6}$-yard long, how many bows can you make with the red spool of ribbon? _____ Write out the division problem and show all the steps.

3. If you want to make white bows that are $\frac{1}{9}$-yard long, how many bows can you make with the white spool of ribbon? _____ Write out the division problem and show all the steps.

4. If you want to make gold bows that are $\frac{2}{7}$-yard long, how many bows can you make with the gold spool of ribbon? _____ Write out the division problem and show all the steps.

Name: _____   Date: _____

Unit 5: Multiplying and Dividing Fractions and Mixed Numbers—Multiplying Mixed Numbers

Let's EXPLORE!

Materials:
- ❑ Crepe paper streamers

Decorating can be fun if you know how to measure. Let's multiply our fun by working through this exploration.

You want to decorate your classroom with streamers of crepe paper and balloons. You have $2\frac{3}{4}$ rolls of streamers to use in the classroom. A small roll of crepe paper streamer is $15\frac{1}{2}$ feet long. Use these mixed numbers to answer the questions.

1. What is the total length of streamer you have?

    A.   First, write out the multiplication problem.

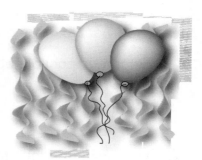

            ☐☐/☐   x   ☐☐/☐

            length of streamer   number of rolls

    B.   Second, rewrite the mixed numbers as improper fractions. Find the numerator of the improper fraction first, and then rewrite the numerator over the same denominator as the mixed number.

        Improper fraction for streamer length:

        ☐   x   ☐   +   ☐   =   ☐

denominator of mixed number	integer of mixed number	numerator of mixed number	numerator of improper fraction

$$\frac{\text{numerator of improper fraction}}{\text{denominator of mixed number}} = \frac{\boxed{}}{\boxed{}}$$

Unit 5: Multiplying and Dividing Fractions and Mixed Numbers—Multiplying Mixed Numbers (cont.)

Improper fraction for the number of rolls:

$$\boxed{} \times \boxed{} + \boxed{} = \boxed{}$$

| denominator of mixed number | integer of mixed number | numerator of mixed number | numerator of improper fraction |

$$\frac{\text{numerator of improper fraction}}{\text{denominator of mixed number}} = \frac{\boxed{}}{\boxed{}}$$

C. Third, multiply the numerators and denominators of the improper fractions.

$$\frac{\boxed{}}{\boxed{}} \times \frac{\boxed{}}{\boxed{}} = \frac{\boxed{}}{\boxed{}}$$

| streamer length | number of rolls |

D. Lastly, rewrite and simplify your answer as a mixed number.

$$\boxed{} \div \boxed{} = \boxed{} \text{ remainder } \boxed{}$$

| numerator of improper fraction | denominator of improper fraction | quotient |

E. Use the quotient, remainder, and denominator of the improper fraction to write how much crepe paper we have as a mixed number.

$$\boxed{}\;\frac{\boxed{}}{\boxed{}}\;\text{remainder}$$

quotient   denominator of improper fraction

F. Break up into groups and decorate your classroom with the streamers.

Let's roll up this exploration by answering this question.

2. Why did we use multiplication to find the total length of crepe paper we had to decorate the classroom? Use complete sentences and write your answer on your own paper.

Unit 5: Multiplying and Dividing Fractions and Mixed Numbers—Multiplying Mixed Numbers (cont.)

Let's EXERCISE!

Writing Improper Fractions as Mixed Numbers

Write the improper fraction represented by the picture and then change it into a mixed number.

1.

2.

_____ = _____   _____ = _____

Multiplying Mixed Numbers

Multiply the mixed numbers by rewriting them as improper fractions. Write your answers as mixed numbers.

3. $1\frac{3}{5} \times 3\frac{2}{3}$ = _____

4. $4\frac{2}{7} \times 9\frac{1}{2}$ = _____

5. $8\frac{1}{3} \times 4\frac{3}{4}$ = _____

6. $2\frac{4}{7} \times 2\frac{5}{7}$ = _____

7. $11\frac{7}{8} \times 1\frac{6}{9}$ = _____

8. $7\frac{5}{6} \times 3\frac{5}{8}$ = _____

Extend Your Knowledge!

9. What change do you make to a whole number when multiplying it by a mixed number?

_____

_____

Unit 5: Multiplying and Dividing Fractions and Mixed Numbers—Multiplying Mixed Numbers (cont.)

Show Your EXPERTISE!

Decorating the Classroom

We want to continue decorating our classroom with streamers. We have $3\frac{2}{5}$ rolls of purple streamer, $1\frac{1}{2}$ rolls of green streamer and $2\frac{2}{3}$ rolls of blue streamer to use for other areas. One small roll of streamer is $15\frac{1}{2}$ feet long. Use the improper fraction to answer the questions.

1. How much of the purple streamer is there to decorate our classroom? _____
   Write out the multiplication problem, and then rewrite it using improper fractions. Write your answer as a mixed number.

2. How much of the green streamer is there to decorate our classroom? _____
   Write out the multiplication problem, and then rewrite it using improper fractions. Write your answer as a mixed number.

3. How much of the blue streamer is there to decorate our classroom? _____
   Write out the multiplication problem, and then rewrite it using improper fractions. Write your answer as a mixed number.

4. What is the total length of all the streamers we have to decorate our classroom?
   _____ Write your answer as a mixed number.

Name: _____ Date: _____

Unit 5: Multiplying and Dividing Fractions and Mixed Numbers—Dividing Mixed Numbers

Let's EXPLORE!

Materials:
- ❑ Roll of newspaper end
- ❑ Markers and crayons

Dive into decorating with banners!

Parent-Teacher conferences are coming up and the class wants to decorate the room with banners and posters welcoming your guests. The teacher has gotten a partial roll of newspaper for the class to cut up into pieces to make banners. The roll is $1\frac{1}{2}$ feet wide and $22\frac{1}{2}$ feet long. Use these measurements to answer the questions.

1. How many $3\frac{1}{4}$-ft. banners can be made out of the roll? Use division to find the answer.

A. First, write out the division problem.

$$\boxed{}\,\frac{\boxed{}}{\boxed{}} \div \boxed{}\,\frac{\boxed{}}{\boxed{}}$$

length of paper   length of one banner

B. Second, rewrite the mixed numbers as improper fractions. Find the numerator of the improper fraction first, and then rewrite the numerator over the same denominator as the mixed number.

Improper fraction for length of the paper:

$$\boxed{} \times \boxed{} + \boxed{} = \boxed{}$$

denominator   integer   numerator   numerator
of mixed   of mixed   of mixed   of improper
number   number   number   fraction

$$\frac{\text{numerator of improper fraction}}{\text{denominator of mixed number}} = \frac{\boxed{}}{\boxed{}}$$

Name: _____ Date: _____

Unit 5: Multiplying and Dividing Fractions and Mixed Numbers—Dividing Mixed Numbers (cont.)

Improper fraction for the length of banners:

☐	x	☐	+	☐	=	☐	

denominator of mixed number   integer of mixed number   numerator of mixed number   numerator of improper fraction

$$\frac{\text{numerator of improper fraction}}{\text{denominator of mixed number}} = \frac{\boxed{}}{\boxed{}}$$

C. Third, invert the second improper fraction and change the division to multiplication.

$$\frac{\boxed{}}{\boxed{}} \times \frac{\boxed{}}{\boxed{}} = \frac{\boxed{}}{\boxed{}}$$

paper length   inverted fraction of banner length

D. Lastly, rewrite and simplify your answer as a mixed number.

☐	÷	☐	=	☐	remainder	☐

numerator of improper fraction   denominator of improper fraction   quotient

E. Use the quotient, remainder, and denominator of the improper fraction to write the mixed number. Then simplify the mixed number.

☐ ☐ remainder

quotient ☐ denominator of improper fraction

F. Break up into groups and make the banners with the measurements from the Exploration.

Let's band together to answer the question below.

2. Why did we use division to find the total number of banners we would have to decorate the classroom with? Use complete sentences and write your answer on your own paper.

79

Name: _____   Date: _____

Unit 5: Multiplying and Dividing Fractions and Mixed Numbers—Dividing Mixed Numbers (cont.)

Let's EXERCISE!

Inverting Mixed Numbers

Write the mixed number as an improper fraction, and then invert it.

1. $5\frac{2}{7}$ _____   _____   2. $3\frac{9}{10}$ _____   _____

3. $10\frac{5}{9}$ _____   _____   4. $8\frac{7}{8}$ _____   _____

Dividing Mixed Numbers

Divide the mixed numbers by rewriting them as improper fractions and multiplying. Write your answers as simplified mixed numbers.

5. $5\frac{2}{3} \div 1\frac{1}{6} =$ _____   6. $8\frac{5}{6} \div 2\frac{1}{9} =$ _____

7. $7\frac{1}{5} \div 3\frac{1}{4} =$ _____   8. $1\frac{7}{8} \div 1\frac{1}{2} =$ _____

Extend Your Knowledge!

9. How do you divide a mixed number by a fraction? Use complete sentences in your answer.

_____

_____

_____

10. Can you divide more than two mixed numbers at a time? _____

Unit 5: Multiplying and Dividing Fractions and Mixed Numbers—Dividing Mixed Numbers (cont.)

Show Your EXPERTISE!

Decorating the School

We want to continue decorating the school by covering bulletin boards with wrapping paper for backgrounds. You have brought in a roll of wrapping paper that is 2 ft. wide by $34\frac{3}{4}$ ft. long to help make backgrounds for the bulletin boards. A fellow classmate has brought in a smaller roll of cellophane wrapping paper measuring 2 ft. wide by $12\frac{1}{2}$ ft. long. Use the mixed numbers to answer the questions.

1. If we keep the width the same on the bigger wrapping paper, how many $4\frac{3}{4}$-ft. long bulletin boards can we cover? Write out the division problem, and then rewrite it using improper fractions and multiplication. Write the answer to the division problem as a mixed number. Then write how many actual bulletin boards we can cover.

   _____

2. If we keep the width the same on the cellophane wrapping paper, how many $3\frac{2}{3}$-ft. long bulletin boards can we cover? Write out the division problem, and then rewrite it using improper fractions and multiplication. Write the answer to the division problem as a mixed number. Then write how many actual bulletin boards we can cover.

   _____

3. If we put both rolls together, how many $3\frac{2}{3}$-ft. long bulletin boards can we cover? Write out the division problem, and then rewrite it using improper fractions and multiplication. Write the answer to the division problem as a mixed number. Then write how many actual bulletin boards we can cover.

   _____

Answer Keys

Unit 1: The Basics
Understanding Fractions
Let's Explore (pages 3–4)
1-11. Answers will vary.
12. Each grape was a separate whole combined with other separate wholes to form a group.
13. Each segment was part of the whole fruit.

Let's Exercise! (page 5)
1. $\frac{3}{6}$ *2.* $\frac{4}{9}$ *3.* $\frac{9}{10}$ *4.* $\frac{5}{11}$ *5.* $\frac{6}{8}$ *6.* $\frac{2}{5}$ *7.* $\frac{9}{12}$ *8.* $\frac{1}{4}$
9-10. Answers will vary.

Show Your Expertise! (page 6)
1-6. Answers will vary.
7. 3   *8.* 7   *9.* 4
10-12. Answers will vary.

Equivalent Fractions
Let's EXPLORE! (pages 7–8)

1. 12   *2.* 6   *3.* $\frac{6}{12}$ *4.* 4   *5.* $\frac{4}{12}$ *6.* 3   *7.* $\frac{3}{12}$
8. Equivalent fractions are fractions that represent the same parts of a whole or group.
9. Answers may vary.

Let's Exercise! (page 9)
1. $\frac{2}{8}, \frac{1}{4}$ *2.* $\frac{2}{4}, \frac{1}{2}$ *3.* $\frac{4}{6}, \frac{2}{3}$ *4.* $\frac{3}{9}, \frac{1}{3}$

5-8. Rectangles may vary. Examples are given.

5. $\frac{2}{5}$    *6.* $\frac{1}{3}$ *7.* $\frac{1}{6}$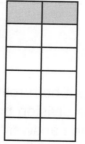

8. $\frac{1}{4}$ 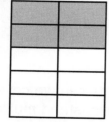   *9.* Answers may vary, but should include that there are an infinite number of equivalent fractions for $\frac{1}{1}$.

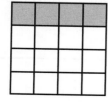

Show Your Expertise! (page 10)

1.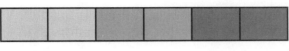

2. $\frac{2}{4}, \frac{1}{2}$

3.

4. $\frac{2}{6}, \frac{1}{3}$

5.

6. $\frac{6}{8}, \frac{3}{4}$

Simplifying Fractions
Let's EXPLORE! (pages 11–12)

1. 36   *2.* 18   *3.* $\frac{18}{36}$ *4.* They are equivalent.   *5.* 18   *6.* 18   *7.* 18

8. 12   *9.* $\frac{12}{36}$ *10.* They are equivalent.   *11.* 12   *12.* 12   *13.* 12

14. Simplified fractions are equivalent to fractions with larger numbers that have common factors.

15. List all the factors of the numerator and denominator, then choose the largest factor.

Let's Exercise! (page 13)

1. 4   *2.* 2   *3.* 5   *4.* 3   *5.* $\frac{3}{4}$ *6.* $\frac{1}{2}$ *7.* $\frac{3}{5}$ *8.* $\frac{1}{3}$

9. The greatest common factor between the numerator and denominator is 1.

Show Your Expertise! (page 14)

1. $\frac{3}{10}$ *2.* $\frac{1}{10}$ *3.* $\frac{4}{25}$ *4.* $\frac{1}{5}$ *5.* $\frac{1}{10}$ *6.* $\frac{7}{50}$ *7.* $\frac{1}{4}$ *8.* $\frac{1}{10}$ *9.* $\frac{1}{10}$

10. $\frac{3}{20}$ *11.* $\frac{2}{5}$

Comparing and Ordering Fractions
Let's EXPLORE! (pages 15–16)

1. 2 yellow, 10 blue, 5 orange, 3 green   *2.* 20

3. yellow: $\frac{2}{20} = \frac{1}{10}$; blue: $\frac{10}{20} = \frac{1}{2}$; orange: $\frac{5}{20} = \frac{1}{4}$; green: $\frac{3}{20} = \frac{3}{20}$

4. blue: $\frac{10}{20} = \frac{1}{2}$ *5.* yellow: $\frac{2}{20} = \frac{1}{10}$ *6.* $\frac{10}{20} > \frac{2}{20}$; $\frac{1}{2} > \frac{1}{10}$

7. The original fractions are easier to compare because when the denominators are the same, you only have to compare the numerators.

8. $\frac{1}{10}, \frac{3}{20}, \frac{1}{4}, \frac{1}{2}$ *9-10.* Answers may vary.

Let's Exercise! (page 17)

1. $\frac{3}{6}; \frac{2}{3}; \frac{3}{6} < \frac{4}{6}$ **2.** $\frac{5}{8}; \frac{3}{4}; \frac{5}{8} < \frac{6}{8}$ **3.** <   **4.** >   **5.** <   **6.** =

7. >   **8.** >   **9.** $\frac{6}{12}, \frac{4}{12}, \frac{1}{12}$ **10.** $\frac{1}{3}, \frac{5}{18}, \frac{2}{9}$ **11.** $\frac{1}{7}, \frac{4}{7}, \frac{6}{7}$

12. $\frac{5}{24}, \frac{3}{8}, \frac{5}{6}$

13. Multiply each fraction's numerator and denominator by the denominator of the other fraction.

Show Your Expertise! (page 18)

1. green   **2.** red   **3.** no   **4.** orange   **5.** purple

6. blue   **7.** green   **8.** blue, orange, brown, green

Unit 2: Adding and Subtracting Fractions
Adding and Subtracting Fractions With Like Denominators
Let's Explore! (pages 20–22)

1. See student's work.   **2.** 28   **3.** Addition

4. $\frac{17}{50}$ **5.** $\frac{11}{50}$ **6.** $\frac{17}{50} + \frac{11}{50} = \frac{28}{50}$ **7.** $\frac{14}{25}$ **8.** 2   **9.** Subtraction

10. $\frac{9}{50}$ **11.** $\frac{7}{50}$ **12.** $\frac{9}{50} - \frac{7}{50} = \frac{2}{50}$ **13.** $\frac{1}{25}$

14. The numerators changed. The numerators were added or subtracted.

15. The denominators stayed the same. The denominators represented the total, so they did not need to change.

Let's Exercise! (page 23)

1. $\frac{1}{4} + \frac{2}{4} = \frac{3}{4}$ **2.** $\frac{3}{5} + \frac{2}{5} = \frac{5}{5} = 1$ **3.** $\frac{3}{5}$ **4.** $\frac{5}{8}$ **5.** $\frac{13}{21}$

6. $\frac{7}{9} - \frac{4}{9} = \frac{3}{9} = \frac{1}{3}$ **7.** $\frac{5}{6} - \frac{4}{6} = \frac{1}{6}$ **8.** $\frac{3}{5}$ **9.** $\frac{4}{11}$ **10.** $\frac{1}{17}$ **11.** a negative one

Show Your Expertise! (pages 24–25)

1. $\frac{7}{36}$ **2.** $\frac{10}{36}$ **3.** $\frac{8}{36}$ **4.** $\frac{9}{36}$ **5.** $\frac{2}{36}$ **6.** $\frac{10}{36} + \frac{8}{36} = \frac{18}{36} = \frac{1}{2}$

7. $\frac{9}{36} + \frac{7}{36} = \frac{16}{36} = \frac{4}{9}$ **8.** $\frac{7}{36} + \frac{10}{36} = \frac{17}{36}$ **9.** $\frac{8}{36} - \frac{2}{36} = \frac{6}{36} = \frac{1}{6}$

10. $\frac{9}{36} - \frac{7}{36} = \frac{2}{36} = \frac{1}{18}$ **11.** $\frac{10}{36} - \frac{9}{36} = \frac{1}{36}$

Finding Common Multiples

Let's Explore! (pages 26–27)

1. Days 2, 4, 6, 8, 10, 12, 14, 16, 18, 20
2. Days 5, 10, 15, 20
3. Days 10 and 20
4. 2, 4, 6, 8, 10, 12, 14, 16, 18, 20
5. The multiples of 2 are the same as the days the map quiz is given.
6. 5, 10, 15, 20, 25, 30, 35, 40, 45, 50
7. The first four multiples of 5 are the same as the days the state capital quiz is given.
8. 10, 20
9. 10
10. The least common multiple of 2 and 5 is the same as the first day that both quizzes were given. The second common multiple is the second day both quizzes were given.
11. Yes; Answers may vary.

Let's Exercise! (page 28)

1. 3, 6, 9, 12, 15, 18, 21, 24   *2.* 4, 8, 12, 16, 20, 24, 28, 32
3. 10, 20, 30, 40, 50, 60, 70, 80   *4.* 12, 24, 36, 48, 60, 72, 84, 96
5. 2, 4, 6, 8, 10, 12, 14, 16   *6.* 9, 18, 27, 36, 45, 54, 63, 72
7. 12   *8.* 70   *9.* 63   *10.* 90   *11.* 28   *12.* 100
13. Answers may vary but could be 40 and 80.
14. Answers may vary but could be 33 and 66.
15. The other number; Answers may vary.

Show Your Expertise! (page 29)

1. 6, 12, 18, 24, 30   *2.* 6   *3.* 6, 12, 18, 24, 30   *4.* 6
5. 6, 12, 18, 24, 30   *6.* 6   *7.* snake   *8.* 30

Adding and Subtracting Fractions With Unlike Denominators

Let's Explore! (pages 30–32)

1. See student's work.   *2.* 2   *3.* 7   *4.* Addition   *5.* 36   *6.* 3

7. $\frac{2}{12} \times \frac{3}{3} = \frac{6}{36}$ *8.* 2   *9.* $\frac{7}{18} \times \frac{2}{2} = \frac{14}{36}$ *10.* $\frac{6}{36} + \frac{14}{36} = \frac{20}{36}$ *11.* $\frac{5}{9}$

12. $\frac{14}{36} - \frac{6}{36} = \frac{8}{36} = \frac{2}{9}$

Let's Exercise! (page 33)

1. $\frac{2}{4} + \frac{2}{8}; \frac{4}{8} + \frac{2}{8} = \frac{6}{8}; \frac{3}{4}$ *2.* $\frac{3}{6} + \frac{1}{3}; \frac{3}{6} + \frac{2}{6} = \frac{5}{6}$ *3.* $\frac{4}{18} + \frac{5}{18} = \frac{9}{18}; \frac{1}{2}$

4. $\frac{4}{24} + \frac{6}{24} = \frac{10}{24}; \frac{5}{12}$ *5.* $\frac{5}{9} - \frac{1}{3}; \frac{5}{9} - \frac{3}{9} = \frac{2}{9}$ *6.* $\frac{4}{6} - \frac{11}{24}; \frac{16}{24} - \frac{11}{24} = \frac{5}{24}$

7. $\frac{9}{14} - \frac{6}{14} = \frac{3}{14}$ *8.* $\frac{10}{12} - \frac{9}{12} = \frac{1}{12}$

9. The least common denominator would be the product of the denominators.

Show Your Expertise! (pages 34–35)

1-4.   See student's work; Answers will vary.

Unit 3: Mixed Numbers
Adding and Subtracting Mixed Numbers With Like Denominators
Let's EXPLORE! (pages 37–40)

2. $\frac{1}{5}$ *3.* $2\frac{1}{5}$ *5.* $\frac{2}{5}$ *6.* $2\frac{2}{5}$ *8.* 4 *9.* 3

10. $4\frac{3}{5}$ *11.* $2\frac{1}{5} + 2\frac{2}{5} = 4\frac{3}{5}$ *13.* $\frac{4}{5}$ *14.* $2\frac{4}{5}$ *17.* $1\frac{1}{5}$

18. $2\frac{4}{5} - 1\frac{3}{5} = 1\frac{1}{5}$

Let's EXERCISE! (page 41)

1. $2\frac{3}{8} + 3\frac{4}{8} = 5\frac{7}{8}$ *2.* $2\frac{5}{6} - 1\frac{4}{6} = 1\frac{1}{6}$ *3.* $4\frac{3}{5}$ *4.* $5\frac{1}{5}$

5. $6\frac{1}{2}$ *6.* $7\frac{2}{3}$ *7.* $6\frac{2}{3}$ *8.* $3\frac{1}{10}$ *9.* $1\frac{2}{3}$ *10.* $5\frac{1}{7}$

11. $8\frac{2}{5}$ *12.* $15\frac{1}{2}$ *13.* $1\frac{1}{7}$ *14.* $1\frac{1}{9}$

Show Your EXPERTISE! (page 42)

1-2.   Answers will vary.   *3.* $1\frac{3}{4}$ inches   *4.* $1\frac{1}{8}$ inches

Adding and Subtracting Mixed Numbers With Unlike Denominators
Let's EXPLORE! (pages 43–47)

1-4.   See student's work.   *5.* 3 *6.* $\frac{4}{16}$ *7.* $\frac{15}{16}$ *8.* $3\frac{15}{16}$

9. $2\frac{1}{4} + 1\frac{11}{16} = 3\frac{15}{16}$

10. See student's work. Two whole acres of pumpkins and two whole acres of corn.

11. 0 *12.* $\frac{2}{8}$ *13.* $\frac{3}{8}$ *14.* $\frac{3}{8}$ *15.* $2\frac{5}{8} - 2\frac{1}{4} = \frac{3}{8}$

16-17.   Answers will vary.

Let's EXERCISE! (page 48)

1. $2\frac{1}{4} + 3\frac{1}{6} = 5\frac{5}{12}$ *2.* $2\frac{4}{5} - 1\frac{1}{3} = 1\frac{7}{15}$ *3.* $6\frac{9}{10}$ *4.* $2\frac{1}{8}$

5. $4\frac{7}{30}$ *6.* $12\frac{20}{21}$ *7.* $3\frac{19}{36}$ *8.* $2\frac{7}{30}$ *9.* $3\frac{5}{12}$ *10.* $5\frac{1}{18}$

11. $7\frac{13}{24}$ *12.* $7\frac{41}{60}$ *13.* $3\frac{13}{24}$ *14.* $9\frac{23}{48}$

Show Your EXPERTISE! (page 49)

1. Pumpkin 3 and Pumpkin 4; $18\frac{9}{20}$ **2.** Pumpkin 1 and Pumpkin 5; $20\frac{17}{24}$

3. $1\frac{7}{40}$ **4.** He forgot to find a common denominator before subtracting.

Unit 4: Mixed Numbers and Improper Fractions
Mixed Numbers and Improper Fractions
Let's EXPLORE! (pages 51–53)

3. 2   **4.** 8 divided by 4 is equal to 2.   **7.** 2   **8.** $\frac{2}{4}$

9. 10 divided by 4 is equal to 2 with a remainder of 2.   **10.** $2\frac{2}{4}$
11. Divide the numerator by the denominator to get the whole number part of the mixed number. Write the remainder over the denominator to get the fractional part of the mixed number.
13. 6   **14.** $\frac{6}{3}$ **15.** 2 times 3 is equal to 6.   **17.** 8

18. $\frac{8}{3}$ **19.** 2 times 3 plus 2 is equal to 8.   **20.** multiplication
21. Multiply the denominator by the whole number and then add the numerator. Write the total over the denominator.

Let's EXERCISE! (page 54)

1. $1\frac{7}{8}$ **2.** $3\frac{1}{3}$ **3.** $3\frac{4}{7}$ **4.** $3\frac{5}{9}$ **5.** $3\frac{3}{5}$

6. $6\frac{2}{3}$ **7.** $5\frac{3}{4}$ **8.** $8\frac{1}{2}$ **9.** $9\frac{1}{2}$ **10.** $4\frac{3}{10}$

11. $\frac{11}{5}$ **12.** $\frac{26}{7}$ **13.** $\frac{17}{9}$ **14.** $\frac{17}{6}$ **15.** $\frac{13}{4}$

16. $\frac{35}{8}$ **17.** $\frac{17}{10}$ **18.** $\frac{23}{10}$ **19.** $\frac{11}{2}$ **20.** $\frac{23}{5}$

Show Your EXPERTISE! (page 55)

1.

Amount	Ingredient	Improper Fraction
$3\frac{3}{4}$ cups	all-purpose flour	$\frac{15}{4}$ cups
$4\frac{1}{2}$ teaspoons	baking powder	$\frac{9}{2}$ teaspoons
$1\frac{1}{8}$ teaspoons	salt	$\frac{9}{8}$ teaspoons
$\frac{1}{2}$ teaspoon	baking soda	$\frac{1}{2}$ teaspoon
$\frac{1}{2}$ cup	shortening	$\frac{1}{2}$ cup

$2\frac{1}{4}$ cups   shredded cheddar cheese $\frac{9}{4}$ cups

$1\frac{3}{4}$ cups   buttermilk $\frac{7}{4}$ cups

2. $1\frac{1}{3}$ cups; Answers should include that you divided the numerator by the denominator to get the whole number and then wrote the remainder over 3 to get the fractional part of the mixed number.

Adding Mixed Numbers With Regrouping
Let's EXPLORE! (pages 56–57)

3. 4   **4.** 1   **5.** $4\frac{1}{3}$ **6.** $3\frac{4}{3}$ **7.** $1\frac{1}{3}$ **8.** $4\frac{1}{3}$

9. They are the same.   **12.** 4   **13.** 1   **14.** $4\frac{1}{4}$ **15.** $3\frac{5}{4}$

16. $1\frac{1}{4}$ **17.** $4\frac{1}{4}$ **18.** They are the same.

19. Use regrouping when the sum contains an improper fraction.

20. When you add, the sum is $6\frac{10}{8}$. Use regrouping to rewrite $\frac{10}{8}$ as $1\frac{2}{8}$. Then add this to 6 to get a sum of $7\frac{2}{8}$, which can be simplified to $7\frac{1}{4}$.

Let's EXERCISE! (page 58)

1. $7\frac{2}{7}$ **2.** $5\frac{2}{5}$ **3.** $8\frac{1}{2}$ **4.** $11\frac{1}{3}$ **5.** $10\frac{2}{3}$

6. $9\frac{3}{5}$ **7.** $10\frac{3}{5}$ **8.** $7\frac{1}{5}$ **9.** $10\frac{1}{2}$ **10.** $13\frac{1}{4}$

11. $6\frac{1}{4}$ **12.** $15\frac{1}{2}$ **13.** $10\frac{5}{24}$ **14.** $12\frac{5}{36}$ **15.** $8\frac{5}{14}$

16. $14\frac{7}{15}$ **17.** $20\frac{1}{2}$ **18.** $13\frac{31}{60}$ **19.** $16\frac{11}{18}$ **20.** $13\frac{11}{21}$

Show Your EXPERTISE! (page 59)

Ingredient	Amount
Water	10 cups
Honey	$9\frac{1}{3}$ tablespoons or 28 teaspoons
Salt	$10\frac{1}{3}$ teaspoons
Bread flour	25 cups
Active dry yeast	$18\frac{9}{14}$ teaspoons
Margarine	10 tablespoons
Dry milk powder	$8\frac{1}{2}$ tablespoons

Subtracting Mixed Numbers With Regrouping
Let's EXPLORE! (pages 60–62)

3. 1   **4.** 2   **5.** $1\frac{2}{4}$ **6.** Answers will vary.   **9.** 1

10. 2   **11.** $1\frac{2}{3}$ **12.** Answers will vary.   **13.** 4   **14.** 4

15. $\frac{5}{4}$ **16.** $3\frac{1}{4} = 2\frac{5}{4}$ **17.** $3\frac{1}{4} - 1\frac{3}{4} = 2\frac{5}{4} - 1\frac{3}{4} = 1\frac{2}{4}$

18. 3   **19.** 3   **20.** $\frac{4}{3}$ **21.** $4\frac{1}{3} = 3\frac{4}{3}$

22. $4\frac{1}{3} - 2\frac{2}{3} = 3\frac{4}{3} - 2\frac{2}{3} = 1\frac{2}{3}$

Let's EXERCISE! (page 63)

1. $5\frac{9}{8}$ **2.** $6\frac{11}{9}$ **3.** $1\frac{7}{6}$ **4.** $8\frac{10}{7}$ **5.** $1\frac{3}{4}$

6. $4\frac{4}{7}$ **7.** $3\frac{2}{5}$ **8.** $7\frac{1}{3}$ **9.** $1\frac{4}{9}$ **10.** $1\frac{1}{2}$

11. $\frac{1}{2}$ **12.** $6\frac{2}{5}$ **13.** $10\frac{7}{8}$ **14.** $7\frac{7}{9}$ **15.** $1\frac{5}{12}$

16. $4\frac{11}{12}$ **17.** $4\frac{7}{24}$ **18.** $4\frac{1}{2}$ **19.** $4\frac{20}{21}$ **20.** $\frac{11}{12}$

Show Your EXPERTISE! (page 64)

1. $2\frac{7}{8} - \frac{1}{2} = 2\frac{3}{8}$ cups   **2.** $1\frac{2}{3} - \frac{1}{2} = 1\frac{1}{6}$ cups   **3.** $2\frac{7}{8} - \frac{5}{6} = 2\frac{1}{24}$ cups

4. Answers will vary but should include the fact that he forgot to find a common denominator.

Unit 5: Multiplying and Dividing Mixed Numbers and Fractions
Multiplying Fractions
Let's EXPLORE! (pages 66–67)

1. **A.** $\frac{5}{9} \times \frac{2}{5}$ **B.** $\frac{5}{9} \times \frac{2}{5} = \frac{10}{45}$ **C.** $\frac{10}{45} = \frac{2}{9}$

2. **A.** $\frac{6}{7} \times \frac{7}{8}$ **B.** $\frac{6}{7} \times \frac{7}{8} = \frac{42}{56}$ **C.** $\frac{42}{56} = \frac{3}{4}$

3. The product of two fractions can be another fraction, a mixed number, or a whole number.

Let's EXERCISE! (page 68)

1. $\frac{4}{6} \times \frac{8}{12} = \frac{32}{72} = \frac{4}{9}$
2. $\frac{1}{4} \times \frac{8}{10} = \frac{8}{40} = \frac{1}{5}$
3. $\frac{6}{154} = \frac{3}{77}$
4. $\frac{6}{39} = \frac{2}{13}$
5. $\frac{15}{32}$
6. $\frac{25}{49}$
7. $\frac{16}{180} = \frac{4}{45}$
8. $\frac{30}{210} = \frac{1}{7}$
9. $\frac{8}{90} = \frac{4}{45}$
10. $\frac{7}{48}$
11. $\frac{70}{450} = \frac{7}{45}$
12. $\frac{16}{51}$

13. 1

Show Your EXPERTISE! (page 69)

1. $\frac{2}{9} \times \frac{7}{9} = \frac{14}{81}$ yard
2. $\frac{5}{7} \times \frac{5}{8} = \frac{25}{56}$ yard
3. $\frac{3}{4} \times \frac{7}{12} = \frac{21}{48} = \frac{7}{16}$ yard
4. $\frac{8}{9} \times \frac{4}{5} = \frac{32}{45}$ yard

Dividing Fractions
Let's EXPLORE! (pages 70–71)

1. A. $\frac{4}{5} \div \frac{1}{6}$ B. $\frac{4}{5} \times \frac{6}{1} = \frac{24}{5}$ C. $\frac{24}{5} = 4\frac{4}{5}$
   D. See student's work. Four towels should be cut.
2. A. $\frac{6}{7} \div \frac{1}{9}$ B. $\frac{6}{7} \times \frac{9}{1} = \frac{54}{7}$ C. $\frac{54}{7} = 7\frac{5}{7}$
   D. See student's work. Seven ribbons should be cut.
3. Yes; Answers may vary.

Let's EXERCISE! (page 72)

1. $\frac{6}{8} \div \frac{1}{4} = \frac{6}{8} \times \frac{4}{1} = \frac{24}{8} = 3$
2. $\frac{4}{5} \div \frac{11}{16} = \frac{4}{5} \times \frac{16}{11} = \frac{64}{55} = 1\frac{9}{55}$
3. $\frac{3}{10} \times \frac{5}{1} = \frac{15}{10} = 1\frac{1}{2}$
4. $\frac{2}{7} \times \frac{14}{5} = \frac{28}{35} = \frac{4}{5}$
5. $\frac{4}{9} \times \frac{13}{12} = \frac{52}{108} = \frac{13}{27}$
6. $\frac{8}{11} \times \frac{3}{2} = \frac{24}{22} = 1\frac{1}{11}$
7. $\frac{13}{15} \times \frac{5}{2} = \frac{65}{30} = 2\frac{1}{6}$
8. $\frac{7}{8} \times \frac{8}{5} = \frac{56}{40} = 1\frac{2}{5}$
9. $\frac{5}{6} \times \frac{4}{3} = \frac{20}{18} = 1\frac{1}{9}$
10. $\frac{6}{10} \times \frac{2}{1} = \frac{12}{10} = 1\frac{1}{5}$

11. 1

Show Your Expertise! (page 73)

1. $\frac{3}{4} \div \frac{3}{8} = \frac{3}{4} \times \frac{8}{3} = \frac{24}{12} = 2$
2. $\frac{2}{3} \div \frac{1}{6} = \frac{2}{3} \times \frac{6}{1} = \frac{12}{3} = 4$
3. $\frac{8}{9} \div \frac{1}{9} = \frac{8}{9} \times \frac{9}{1} = \frac{72}{9} = 8$
4. $\frac{6}{7} \div \frac{2}{7} = \frac{6}{7} \times \frac{7}{2} = \frac{42}{14} = 3$

Multiplying Mixed Numbers
Let's EXPLORE! (pages 74–75)

1. **A.** $15\frac{1}{2} \times 2\frac{3}{4}$ **B.** $2 \times 15 + 1 = 31; \frac{31}{2}; 4 \times 2 + 3 = 11; \frac{11}{4}$ **C.** $\frac{31}{2} \times \frac{11}{4} = \frac{341}{8}$

D. $341 \div 8 = 42 \text{ r } 5$ **E.** $42\frac{5}{8}$

2. Answers may vary.

Let's EXERCISE! (page 76)

1. $\frac{17}{6} = 2\frac{5}{6}$ **2.** $\frac{13}{4} = 3\frac{1}{4}$ **3.** $\frac{8}{5} \times \frac{11}{3} = \frac{88}{15}; 5\frac{13}{15}$

4. $\frac{30}{7} \times \frac{19}{2} = \frac{570}{14}; 40\frac{5}{7}$ **5.** $\frac{25}{3} \times \frac{19}{4} = \frac{475}{12}; 39\frac{7}{12}$ **6.** $\frac{18}{7} \times \frac{19}{7} = \frac{342}{49}; 6\frac{48}{49}$

7. $\frac{95}{8} \times \frac{15}{9} = \frac{1425}{72} = 19\frac{19}{24}$ **8.** $\frac{47}{6} \times \frac{29}{8} = \frac{1363}{48} = 28\frac{19}{48}$

9. The whole number needs to be made into a fraction by making it have a denominator of 1.

Show Your EXPERTISE! (page 77)

1. $3\frac{2}{5} \times 15\frac{1}{2} = \frac{17}{5} \times \frac{31}{2} = \frac{527}{10} = 52\frac{7}{10}$ feet

2. $1\frac{1}{2} \times 15\frac{1}{2} = \frac{3}{2} \times \frac{31}{2} = \frac{93}{4} = 23\frac{1}{4}$ feet

3. $2\frac{2}{3} \times 15\frac{1}{2} = \frac{8}{3} \times \frac{31}{2} = \frac{248}{6} = 41\frac{2}{6} = 41\frac{1}{3}$ feet

4. $117\frac{17}{60}$ feet

Dividing Mixed Numbers
Let's EXPLORE! (pages 78–79)

1. **A.** $22\frac{1}{2} \div 3\frac{1}{4}$ **B.** $2 \times 22 + 1 = 45; \frac{45}{2}; 4 \times 3 + 1 = 13; \frac{13}{4}$

C. $\frac{45}{2} \times \frac{4}{13} = \frac{180}{26}$ **D.** $180 \div 26 = 6 \text{ r } 24$ **E.** $6\frac{24}{26} = 6\frac{12}{13}$

2. Answers may vary.

Let's EXERCISE! (page 80)

1. $\dfrac{37}{7}$; $\dfrac{7}{37}$ **2.** $\dfrac{39}{10}$; $\dfrac{10}{39}$ **3.** $\dfrac{95}{9}$; $\dfrac{9}{95}$ **4.** $\dfrac{71}{8}$; $\dfrac{8}{71}$

5. $\dfrac{17}{3} \div \dfrac{7}{6}$; $\dfrac{17}{3} \times \dfrac{6}{7} = \dfrac{102}{21} = 4\dfrac{6}{7}$ **6.** $\dfrac{53}{6} \div \dfrac{19}{9}$; $\dfrac{53}{6} \times \dfrac{9}{19} = \dfrac{477}{114} = 4\dfrac{7}{38}$

7. $\dfrac{36}{5} \div \dfrac{13}{4}$; $\dfrac{36}{5} \times \dfrac{4}{13} = \dfrac{144}{65} = 2\dfrac{14}{65}$ **8.** $\dfrac{15}{8} \div \dfrac{3}{2}$; $\dfrac{15}{8} \times \dfrac{2}{3} = \dfrac{30}{24} = 1\dfrac{1}{4}$

9. The mixed number should be changed into an improper fraction. Then invert the fraction and multiply.

10. No

Show Your EXPERTISE! (page 81)

1. $34\dfrac{3}{4} \div 4\dfrac{3}{4} = \dfrac{139}{4} \div \dfrac{19}{4}$; $\dfrac{139}{4} \times \dfrac{4}{19} = \dfrac{556}{76} = 7\dfrac{6}{19}$; 7 boards

2. $12\dfrac{1}{2} \div 3\dfrac{2}{3} = \dfrac{25}{2} \div \dfrac{11}{3}$; $\dfrac{25}{2} \times \dfrac{3}{11} = \dfrac{75}{22} = 3\dfrac{9}{22}$; 3 boards

3. $47\dfrac{1}{4} \div 3\dfrac{2}{3} = \dfrac{189}{4} \div \dfrac{11}{3}$; $\dfrac{189}{4} \times \dfrac{3}{11} = \dfrac{567}{44} = 12\dfrac{39}{44}$; 12 boards